BONACINA

BONACINA

THE BEAUTY OF RATTAN

TEXT BY MARELLA CARACCIOLO CHIA
PHOTOGRAPHY BY GUIDO TARONI

FOREWORD BY MADISON COX
INTRODUCTION BY ELIA BONACINA

Rizzoli
NEW YORK

New York · Paris · London · Milan

CONTENTS

FOREWORD

Madison Cox

As a boy growing up in California in the late 1960s and early 1970s, one of a multitude of influences in my young life was my uncle, San Francisco–based artist David Ireland. With his stylish wife, Joanne, Ireland had a shop called Hunter Africa, on then-fashionable Union Street, where he introduced an affluent market to objects sourced mainly from the African continent. I remember so vividly the warehouse-like gallery space, as it was a glimpse into an exciting and exotic world that Ireland had experienced firsthand as a young man in his twenties when he went off on a yearlong journey through Kenya. Tribal drums, Maasai spears, vivid textiles, wood-carved ritual masks, and multicolored glass-beaded neck collars were interspersed with furniture that filled the cavernous space. One of the furniture lines he produced was made of rattan in Hong Kong: some pieces ended up furnishing our family's summer cabin in the San Juan Islands off the coast of the Pacific Northwest. Ireland's passion for rattan ultimately translated into an art piece—a pair of oversize wicker armchairs made of Palembang cane titled *South China Chairs* (1979)—that is held today in the permanent collection of the San Francisco Museum of Modern Art. These pieces became iconic for me; a deep souvenir, if not a remembrance, of my San Francisco childhood.

Fast-forward some decades later: while I was working on a garden project in Morocco for the late Marella Agnelli, I recall that during our numerous conversations, she too spoke of her passion for rattan furniture, which was also linked to her childhood memories. Agnelli's father, a member of the Italian diplomatic service, was posted in various locations; her American-born mother, Margaret Clarke, was often called upon to speedily furnish rented houses for diplomatic postings or summer residences. She would often furnish these temporary lodgings with wicker furniture, as it was readily available and relatively inexpensive. For Agnelli, rattan furniture became a token of her childhood, and in turn became a trademark of sorts throughout her life. The manufacturer she would return to over the decades was the Italian family firm Bonacina.

The art of furniture produced from plant materials is centuries old; examples made of woven canes, reeds, and fronds can be found throughout the world, from East Asia to India, the Middle East, and the Gulf States—which still produce palm frond furniture—to Europe and the Americas.

Since 1889, the name synonymous with rattan furniture is Bonacina, the venerable company run by generations of the same family. Based on the shores of Lake Como, north of Milan, four generations of the Bonacina family have worked for more than a century with some of the most influential designers and architects to produce some of the iconic furniture pieces of modern times.

In a world of mass production and cookie-cutter uniformity, Bonacina's unique vision and quest for superiority in handcraftsmanship has led the firm to shine above so many others. Twentieth-century design maestros and architects, including Franco Albini, Gae Aulenti, Renzo Mongiardino, and Gio Ponti collaborated and have become synonymous with Bonacina, as have contemporary masters such as Mattia Bonetti and Francis Sultana, who continue the grand tradition of working with the Italian company.

The Bonacina heritage of superior quality and craftsmanship has been carefully passed down from generation to generation of workers at the company; the furniture and objects they produce symbolize an excellence that is unique in the annals of design and decoration. They are, in the truest sense, timeless.

I feel privileged to have known the Bonacina family for nearly thirty years, a friendship that began when I first visited their storerooms filled with what seemed to be a sample of every piece they had ever designed. What I'll always retain from that most rewarding visit, after examining the vast range of pieces produced by Bonacina and considering the creative impulse behind every one of them, is the vital importance that handmade pieces such as these must continue to play in today's world. This invaluable book chronicles a family's passion that has carried on through four generations and will undoubtedly continue to flourish onward, into the future.

INTRODUCTION

Elia Bonacina

A warm greeting to all those beginning to read this book about my family's history, our company's legacy of exquisite design and artistry, and the elegance of living with rattan furniture. As president and chief executive officer, and as a representative of the fourth generation of the Bonacina family from Lurago d'Erba, whose members have been working in the design world since 1889, I wanted to share a few words about the magic of this company before you embark on your journey into the rare beauty and sophistication that every page of this book holds.

I was born in the nineteenth-century villa built by Giovanni Bonacina, the patriarch of our dynasty. As was customary in Brianza at the time, the villa was adjoined to the company's main workshop (*ca' e botega*), so, right from the start, I experienced the sounds of the factory, the scent of rattan, and the dynamism of the company's production. Inside the factory, I developed my senses of touch, sight, and smell, and, as I grew up, these became refined, enabling me to recognize every type of rattan, discern any aniline, natural, or lacquered color, and learn from our employees the art of taming rattan with fire to transform it into surprising new shapes. To me, at the time, it was like seeing Indiana Jones fighting with an anaconda—a feat of rare artistry every time.

Upon waking, I couldn't wait to step onto the factory floor to enjoy the spectacle, and I always felt so lucky and grateful for who I was, where I'd been born, and what my family did for a living. I learned early on how to correctly insert a nail into a rattan frame and how to weave rattan core. The employees of my grandparents, Vittorio and Carla, and then of my parents, Mario and Antonia, have always been part of my family. I've spent so much time with them—laughing, joking, working, and talking seriously about life—that they couldn't help but affect who I am. For an entrepreneur in Brianza—which is, incidentally, one of the most densely industrialized places in the world— business, family, and home are historically entwined into a single entity. Although certainly not always a simple way to live, in our case it paved the way to great satisfaction.

It's an honor and a privilege for me, at the age of thirty-three, to guide this company, which is an undisputed global leader and an emblem of design history, representing and glorifying a manufacturing tradition that a family, workers, and a specific territory have carried forward from generation to generation for over a century. Such dedication, as you will see in this book, has enabled the company to cross paths with some of the world's most famous and sophisticated people. Bonacina can thus count on several extremely prestigious designers, whose collaborations have enabled many of our works a place in the world's most illustrious books on decoration and design and in many important museums.

Over the last twelve years, since I've been leading the firm, we've shown how it is possible to keep a company fresh and dynamic even after 135 years of history. To me, there is no future without the present and no present without the past. Today, Bonacina continues to interweave these three concepts—past, present, and future—as it moves forward, also bestowing them on its products, both aesthetically and productively.

Ours is one of the most ancient manufacturing traditions in Europe, relying on discipline and following specific rules that have enabled it to continue to live gloriously over time. Our products are made entirely by hand. No machines are used in any of our processes. Our employees make the products in the exact same way as my great-grandfather Giovanni Bonacina did. With a waiting list that can sometimes extend up to several months, our customers patiently anticipate a product that they know will be unique, which will become part of their personal histories and families. Ultimately, these are furnishing items on which we cry, laugh, rejoice, and watch the seasons pass. As Margherita—my sister, business partner, and product art director—says, these are objects that accompany us through life and that we grow fond of.

Our works acquire value over time, as shown by the numerous auction houses throughout the world that sell them for two to three times the original purchase price. To me, "Made in Italy" has become a much more complex designation than a label affixed to a product. It is something that can be seen, felt, and inhaled, and has to do with the story, territory, and unique atmospheres of this country, which in its 2,000-year history, continues to shape the aesthetics and culture of products.

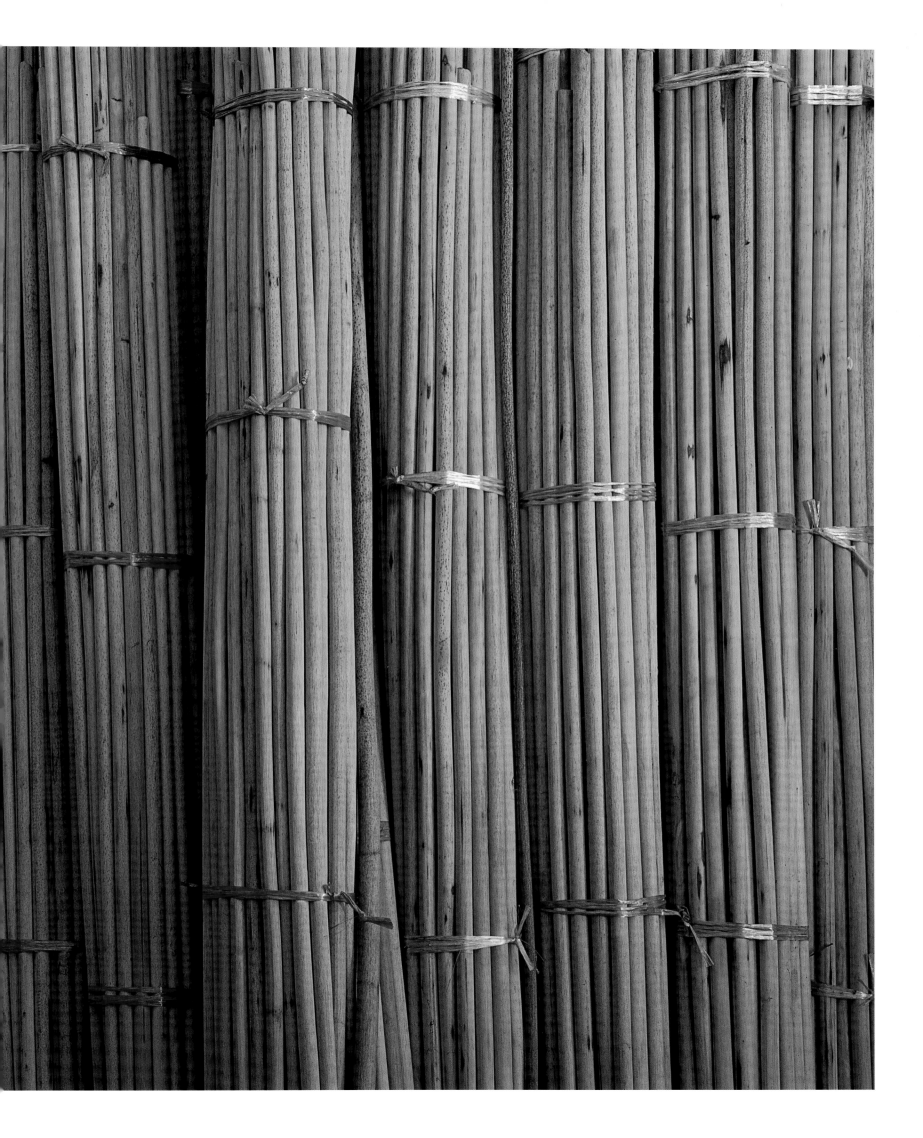

I.
INTERIORS

Living with the Beauty of Rattan

Passalacqua
Lake Como

"Passalacqua is an eighteenth-century villa on the shores of Lake Como that was originally built to host the annual renewal of body and spirit known as *la villeggiatura*. We have restored this artistic jewel and made it the venue for a new kind of renewal, one that is open to cultured globetrotters while firmly rooted in the authentic values of the past.

It is uncanny how well the furnishings, which we chose together with Bonacina for the villa and its terraced gardens, express this spirit. Many, such as the *Antica* chair in our *Sala delle Dame* dining room, or the *978* chairs on the bar terrace, derive from a collaboration between Mario Bonacina and the great Italian interior designer Renzo Mongiardino, which was all about giving models from the firm's historical archive new vigor while staying true to its values of fine artisanship and old-school elegance—an approach that is dear to our heart here at Passalacqua! We also have more contemporary Bonacina pieces, such as the *Margherita* armchairs, designed by Franco Albini, that work so beautifully in our colorful winter garden, a former greenhouse repurposed by the flamboyant designer J. J. Martin from La Double J.

We love Bonacina's attention to detail and the dynamism of its designs, but that's not the only reason we feel a great affinity with this exalted firm. It is in the province of Como, just like us; the company, like us, is connected to the summer exodus of the great Milanese families (which created a demand for elegant alfresco furniture); and just like us, it is a proud family-owned company. For us that's a real source of strength and solid values.

PAOLO, ANTONELLA, AND VALENTINA DE SANTIS

Mondadori Residence
Milan

"I grew up surrounded by Bonacina chairs, so when I established my first home, I naturally wanted to re-create the environment in which I'd felt good—like a sort of Proust madeleine."

MARTINA MONDADORI

"Here are some of my memories related to the Mondadori family house in Milan, a project we worked on from the late 1970s into the early '80s. The design of the house was a collaboration with architect Renzo Mongiardino and Paola Zanussi Mondadori.

From the entrance, the long corridor with its trompe-l'oeil library, meticulously hand-painted according to Mongiardino's vision, becomes one of the most iconic points of the house: it is here, at the end of the space, that we placed the *May Fair* armchairs.

The dining room is a place of convergence, with the dining chairs that give a distinctive light touch, emphasizing the intrinsic value of the material. In the living room, next to the fireplace, the *Astrea* armchairs, born from our collaboration with Mongiardino, lend timeless elegance.

The terrace has undergone a transformation over the years; today, outdoor furniture upholstered in finely sourced textiles enhances the space, creating a welcoming and refined atmosphere.

This residence stands as a testament to Mongiardino's vision—a masterpiece that not only speaks of extraordinary beauty but also resonates with the warmth of the family."

MARIO BONACINA

Mattia Bonetti Residence
Lake Lugano

"Having been born and raised on the shores of Lake Lugano in Switzerland and thus steeped in and permeated by Italianness, it was almost destiny, or perhaps a lucky twist of fate, when I one day met the Bonacina tribe. Hailing from a town near Lake Como, they came to weave a friendship with me, in addition to a professional relationship.

And, since I've mentioned the notion of *weaving*, who was and still is today the sublime proponent, always coming out on top, of this high-level craft from time immemorial, whose intrinsic traits have enabled it to thrive in three different centuries?

The Bonacina clan: precisely Mario and Antonia and the next generation, Elia and Margherita.

It is indisputably a primitive human activity, and indeed seems so simple and natural, to thread horizontal segments through other vertical ones, thus coming to create a new entity from practically nothing—a material that in Bonacina's case is a plant-based mesh but that is also and above all a product of people and human stories.

I wish and hope for them and myself, but also for those still to come, that all this may continue for a long time, across the ages, step by step, leaving a mark of their unmistakable journey."

MATTIA BONETTI

Agnelli Residence, Aïn Kassimou
Marrakech

"Bonacina chairs have always been part of my world! First in my grandmother's houses—whether in the mountains, at the beach, or in the city, different versions were always present—then, in my mother's residence and, finally, my own. To me, they are the most comforting, familiar items of furniture, and they make me feel at home."

GINEVRA ELKANN

"The Aïn Kassimou house, dating back to the late nineteenth century and acquired by Marella Agnelli in 2003, has been a source of professional joy for me. It was Gae Aulenti who introduced me to this extraordinary project while working on a section of it.

This marked the long-lasting collaboration with Marella, a relationship that I still cherish in the memories of those days spent together in her mountain home in St. Moritz designing this new house.

I remember Marella as a confident and determined woman, endowed with exceptional taste. During visits to choose furnishings, I stood by her side in a respectful manner, seeking to grasp her unique and refined vision.

During one of these visits, the idea to design a special, unique chair for this residence came to us. An idea that, until now, has never been given an official name, but in her honor, we will call it the "Marella Chair." This creation is a tribute to her elegance and the ability to transform structural elements into light and silent decorations.

A distinctive element, serving as a *fil rouge* (in the true sense of the term), is the bicolor weave with vermilion-lacquered rattan core thread. This specific weave, alternating with Tea aniline-stained threads, became a stylistic signature present in many of her homes, including her apartment in New York. A detail that added a personal firm and unique touch to the environment, transforming spaces into works of art."

MARIO BONACINA

BRANDO BICOLOR Dining chairs, 1975
Mario Bonacina, inspired by the Bonacina
Historical Archive
pages 49, 50–51, 55

CROCHET Sofa, 1973
Mario Bonacina and Renzo Mongiardino
pages 50–51, 56–57

Custom coffee table, 1973
Mario Bonacina and Renzo Mongiardino
pages 50–51, 52–53

LISIPPO Dining chairs, 1974
Mario Bonacina and Renzo Mongiardino
page 54

1925/1 Dining chairs, 1979
Gae Aulenti, inspired by the Bonacina
Historical Archive
pages 56–57, 64

BOURLON Sofa, 1973
Mario Bonacina and Renzo Mongiardino
pages 56–57

MARELLA Custom chairs, 2004
Mario Bonacina
pages 58–59, 60–61, 63

VIOLET Armchairs, 1973
Mario Bonacina and Renzo Mongiardino
pages 60–61

1925/1 Ottoman, 1979
Gae Aulenti, inspired by the Bonacina
Historical Archive
pages 60–61

DAMA Dining chairs, 2005
Mario Bonacina
page 62

BRANDO BICOLOR Custom chairs, 1975
Mario Bonacina, inspired by the Bonacina
Historical Archive
pages 66–67, 68, 69

The Jardin Majorelle
Marrakech

"Both the Jardin Majorelle and its neighboring Villa Oasis have been extraordinary sources of inspiration not only for their founder and namesake, the French painter Jacques Majorelle, but also for the French couturier Yves Saint Laurent, who, together with his partner Pierre Bergé, deserve so much credit for having saved these unique properties for posterity.

The same passion is felt at the family firm of Bonacina, where the finest in workmanship and innovation in their field of handcrafted furniture has been transmitted from generation to generation.

The brilliant young Italian photographer Guido Taroni has taken images for this book that capture the magical atmosphere at the one-of-a-kind Jardin Majorelle, a quality that captivates the numerous visitors from around the world who discover it.

In a world of mass standardization and conformity, both Bonacina and the Jardin Majorelle exemplify the vital importance of supporting and preserving these sorts of institutions that embrace passionate individual expression. It is therefore with great respect and sincere acknowledgment that I salute the entire Bonacina family and wish them continued success in all of their remarkable endeavors."

MADISON COX

ARPA Armchairs, 1985
Mario Bonacina and Renzo Mongiardino
pages 73, 74–75

1925/5 Dining chairs, 1980
Mario Bonacina
pages 79, 88–89

978 Chairs, 1975
Mario Bonacina and Renzo Mongiardino
pages 80–81, 88–89

Le Sirenuse
Positano

"When we decided, in the late 1980s, to create a new bar called Aldo's for Le Sirenuse, on an unused terrace, the first thought my father had was to go and see Bonacina to select all the outdoor furniture. He had seen the company's designs at Villa d'Este and had fallen in love with the beauty and incredible craftsmanship.

He chose a sofa by Renzo Mongiardino. The sofa was originally designed to accommodate two people; my father, however, decided to have it made just a little smaller, ensuring that the unaware occupants would naturally end up embracing each other! And so our Aldo's bar came to life, with soft lights, the sound of the sea in the distance, and the artfully made Bonacina furniture gently guaranteeing that you will always be embracing your loved one. 'Ahhh,' I think each time I walk by the bar, 'if only these sofas could recount the stories they've heard.'"

ANTONIO SERSALE

ASTREA Dining chairs, 1977
Mario Bonacina and Renzo Mongiardino
pages 92–93

CHAMPAGNE BAR Armchairs, 1975
Mario Bonacina and Renzo Mongiardino
pages 92–93

Custom table, 1985
Mario Bonacina and Renzo Mongiardino
pages 92–93

Federico Forquet Residence
Cetona

"I can't mention Bonacina without conjuring three words in my mind: friendship, talent, and quality—and these remain forever.

My first encounter with Mario Bonacina dates back to the early 1970s. At that time, Gianni and Marella Agnelli had an apartment in the Grand Hotel for their stays in Rome, furnished for them by Stéphane Boudin, but it wouldn't last much longer. Marella, who wasn't a fan of hotels, had found a magnificent apartment with a view overlooking the whole city and its ancient domes.

The plans had begun and that was why Mario was in Rome. He had brought with him drawings and photographs of items he'd made, and I was immediately won over by this type of furniture I didn't have much knowledge of until then.

Following that meeting, in every home or place I've inhabited, a 'Bonacina' has always been present. With Mario and Antonia, there is extraordinary collaboration and harmony, such that even projects explained over the phone are perfectly interpreted. It's no coincidence that while writing these fond memories, I'm comfortably relaxed on a rattan-core chaise longue painted black and commissioned in 1973. You wouldn't believe it's fifty years old and still perfect and that I'm still very happy with it!

I feel like that says it all about Bonacina's work."

FEDERICO FORQUET

MAISON & JARDIN HORS SÉRIE N° 11   JARDINS
MAISON & JARDIN HORS SÉRIE N° 17   JARDINS
MAISON & JARDIN HORS SÉRIE N° 14   JARDINS
MAISON & JARDIN HORS SÉRIE N° 8   JARDINS

DM 17 / FB 255 / Ptas 780 / Lit. 8000 / FS 12.5 / US $ 8.95 / FF 35
DM 17 / FB 255 / Ptas 780 / Lit. 8000 / FS 12.5 / US $ 8.95 / FF 35
DM 17 / FB 255 / Ptas 780 / Lit. 8000 / FS 12.5 / US $ 8.95 / FF 35
DM 17 / FB 255 / Ptas 780 / Lit. 8000 / FS 12.5 / US $ 8.95 / FF 35

Lauder Residence
Wainscott

"Bonacina epitomizes style and elegance. The timeless beauty and wonderful quality make the pieces true works of art."

AERIN LAUDER

"While designing the sitting room in Aerin's house in Wainscott, New York, I was inspired by the porches of the early twentieth-century houses of Charles A. Platt, particularly Woodston in Mount Kisco. What is so nice about this room is that the furniture arrangement is composed of two identical groupings, and Bonacina's woven pieces really make it feel like an outdoor space."

DANIEL ROMUALDEZ

905 Dining chairs, 1970
Alberto Colombi
pages 112–13, 114

CROCHET Sofas and armchairs, 1973
Mario Bonacina and Renzo Mongiardino
pages 112–13, 114, 115

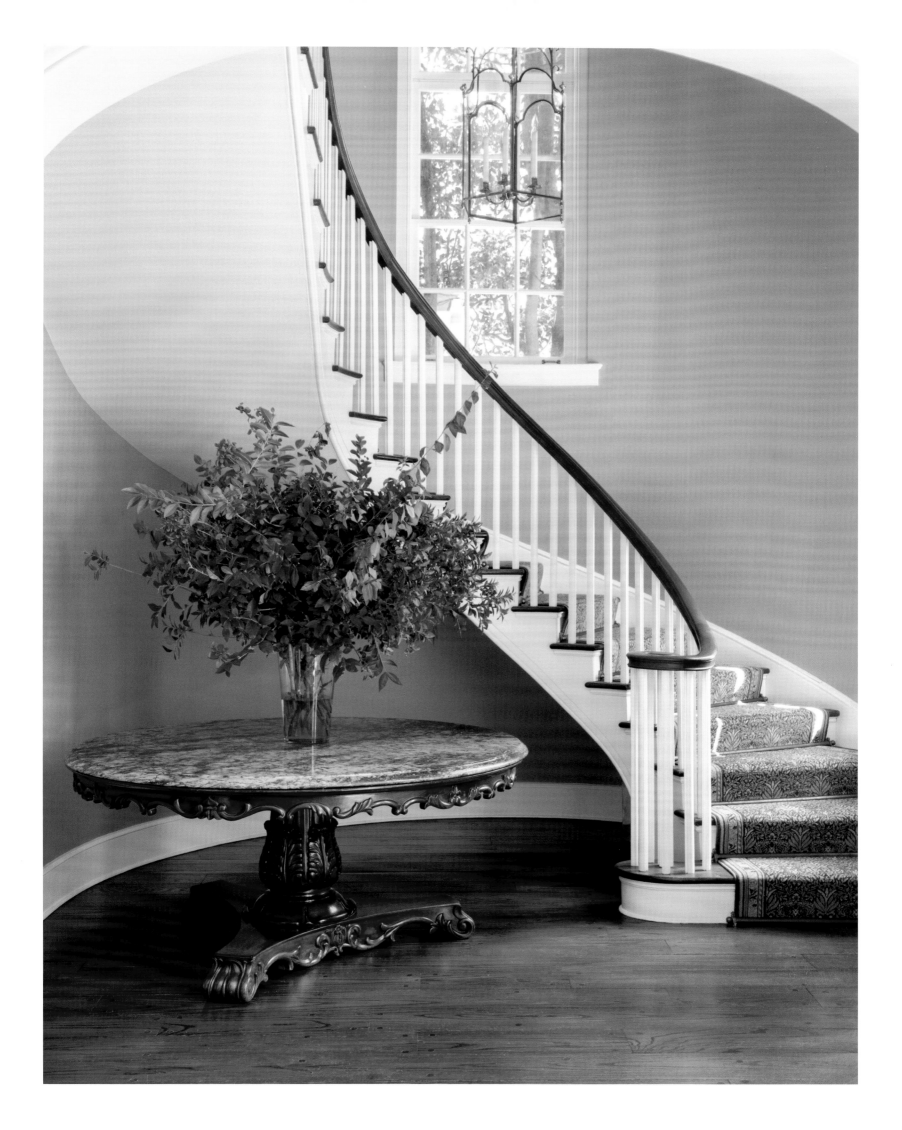

Hotel Cala di Volpe
Costa Smeralda

"Soft and docile, but also strong and resistant, rattan is the lightest and most authentic material we know. It lets in light, which is always at the heart of our work, and casts changing shadows on walls and floors. We love it. And we love it above all when Bonacina works and shapes it.

When we were commissioned to renovate the legendary Hotel Cala di Volpe on the Emerald Coast, we immediately planned to use rattan. The weaving tradition in Sardinia was still vibrant when Jacques Couëlle designed the hotel in the early 1960s, and he had already used the material. It felt natural for us to use it for the furniture in certain strategic areas of the hotel. For the atrium, the hotel's true beating heart, it was an obvious choice: the honey-colored rattan curves of the deep armchairs in this winter garden echo the ochre and white masonry arches cutting through the sea view. As for the braided patterns on the backrests, which we designed to resemble radiant suns, they add a cheerful, optimistic note throughout the day.

The design and manufacture of this furniture carried immense importance, as it had to embody absolute quality and unrivaled design: we couldn't go wrong in our choice of partner. Bonacina, the last of the great craftspeople who continue to think, invent, and dream with rattan, was the cornerstone of our work from the beginning, allowing us to unleash our creativity. The project with Antonia, Mario, and the entire Bonacina team was a magnificent adventure, a true collaboration. And in the final result, we no longer wonder who came up with what, since our ideas have mutually contributed so much to each other.

Ultimately, what brought us the greatest joy with Bonacina was to perpetuate a centuries-old tradition while projecting ourselves into the future. We're always rewarded when we play the game of authenticity."

CLAIRE BÉTAILLE AND BRUNO MOINARD OF MOINARD BÉTAILLE

Villa Feltrinelli
Lake Garda

"I like a room that is alive, in which furniture from different periods and genres mingles together. Museums can hold the period rooms. Bonacina, with its profiles and its natural rattan, brings us furniture that mixes effortlessly with others and that makes a room more interesting and eclectic. The history, the artisan's hand, and the designs combine to strengthen it—pure perfection.

So many of my favorite Italian architects worked with Bonacina.

Renzo Mongiardino's *Astrea* chair in black, with that distinctive pointy profile and small scale, seemed perfect for the Villa Feltrinelli. In the main, mirrored salon, its dark profile stands straight-backed, at attention, mingling with lounge chairs and banquettes original to the villa. The balance is perfect for a formal room in an Italian lakeside villa. The dark rattan next to the white slipcovered classics is a living example of my desire for a room that does not sit quietly in an era, that is alive with several centuries of design and style. On the adjoining terrace, the companion settee provides the perfect setting for an evening prosecco.

In the villa's boathouse, a more casual apartment on the lake, the dining room setting is reminiscent of Van Day Truex's house in Provence. In the more modernist living room, a pair of *Siesta* lounge chairs—recently designed and larger in scale—sits as sculpture flanking the fireplace. The perfect setting for a *Siesta*.

Impeccable quality and joyful to the eyes . . . my impression of Bonacina."

PAMELA BABEY OF BAMO

BRANDO BICOLOR Outdoor dining
chairs, 1975
Mario Bonacina, inspired by the Bonacina
Historical Archive
page 129

ASTREA Dining chairs, 1977
Mario Bonacina and Renzo Mongiardino
pages 130–31

SIESTA Armchairs, 2010
Mattia Bonetti
pages 132–33

Da Giacomo Arengario
Milan

"It's owing to our teacher, the architect Renzo Mongiardino, that we have known and worked with Bonacina for more than thirty years. To us, the name has always been a byword for uncontrived elegance, not necessarily tied to the garden and outdoors but, rather, suited to balancing the opulence of an interior with a touch of nonchalance. Pairing silk- and damask-upholstered sofas and armchairs with rattan chairs designed for an interior has enabled us to create harmonious contrasts that have always given our projects a certain lightness.

In the case of Da Giacomo Arengario restaurant in Piazza Duomo, we designed a veranda inside the overhanging loggia created by Piero Portaluppi in the late 1930s. Made of iron and glass, our construction could not exceed or dominate the architecture of the site, but needed to appear almost like the bow of a yacht stretching out into the square, toward the windows of the cathedral. Together with Bonacina, we designed the seating based on this vision: rattan armchairs, chairs, and sofas, imagining them as items of furniture salvaged from a yacht of that earlier time. The guests of the restaurant had to be able to sit comfortably and at ease in a classic atmosphere while enjoying a surprising view, which is arguably one of Milan's most beautiful.

The chairs have arched legs that allude to the arches of the loggia and continue the metaphysical simplification of architecture of that period, rigorous horizontal and diagonal lines grafted onto those of the veranda, densely woven rattan core, and are amber colored with oxblood linen cushions. Surrounding the circular and rectangular tables, which are painted in black varnish with glass tops edged with a coated metal ferrule, the chairs take on the starring role."

ROBERTO PEREGALLI AND LAURA SARTORI RIMINI OF STUDIO PEREGALLI SARTORI

Custom chairs, 2010
Studio Peregalli Sartori
with Mario Bonacina
pages 135, 136–37

Hotel La Palma
Capri

"Bonacina stands for everything I love about Italian design. A family company that has been creating woven furniture since 1889, it has a history that represents beauty, quality, and true sophistication. A piece by Bonacina is beyond trends and fashions.

I have worked with Bonacina for more than two decades. In all my residential projects, and now in my hotel and restaurant projects, Bonacina is so important to my aesthetic. I have been filled with pride to see my own designs come to life under the expert guidance of Bonacina. The firm is a true inspiration and a great legacy."

FRANCIS SULTANA

Bulgari Hotel
Rome

"I felt the greatest thrill and surprise upon visiting the Bonacina factory in Lurago d'Erba for the first time and seeing a manufacturing site with no machinery. Each person there is devoted to a product based on his or her specific talent and shapes the rattan with great skill and confidence.

　　The older craftspeople teach the younger ones, and everyone feels like they are part of something bigger, something that was around before they were, and that, thanks to them, will continue to exist.

　　For the Bulgari Hotel in Rome, we chose Bonacina because the hotel is a tribute to Italian creativity—our natural bent for excellence and our deepest roots."

ROBERTO MARIANI, SENIOR PROJECT DIRECTOR
ACPV ARCHITECTS ANTONIO CITTERIO PATRICIA VIEL

EVA Armchairs, 1965
Giovanni Travasa
pages 152–53

EXAGONAL Coffee tables, 1981
Mario Bonacina and Renzo Mongiardino
pages 152–53, 155

1925/1 Dining chairs, 1979
Gae Aulenti, inspired by the
Bonacina Historical Archive
page 154

1925/4 Chairs, 1980
Mario Bonacina
pages 154, 156–57

ARPA Armchairs, 1985
Mario Bonacina and Renzo Mongiardino
page 155

Grand Park Hotel
Rovinj

"Bonacina has worked with great masters and has a catalog that crosses all the eras of Italian design since the late nineteenth century. When I began working with the company many years ago, my collaboration was very silent as I designed several objects for them. I interpreted my outdoor collections, sofas, and chairs in keeping with Bonacina's classical school of thought, adding slightly different materials and trying to somehow comply with the company's desire to enter the contemporary sphere.

Having, as they do, one of the world's most beautiful product ranges, it's natural for me to choose from their catalog in my work as an architect. Selecting, above all, pieces designed by the great masters."

PIERO LISSONI

Roberto Agostinelli Residence
Palm Beach

Over the span of nearly four decades, the trajectories of Bonacina and Jacques Grange have converged. With a sense of appreciation, Jacques Grange has willingly provided a collection of photographs that intimately portray the distinctive character of some of his most exceptional interior designs, seamlessly intertwined with pieces by Bonacina.

Grange's unwavering commitment to his craft has not only molded physical spaces but also imprinted an enduring influence on the core of design itself.

CROCHET Sofas and armchairs, 1973
Mario Bonacina and Renzo Mongiardino
pages 167, 168–69

Palazzo Margherita
Bernalda

Palazzo Margherita, constructed in 1892 in Bernalda by the Margherita family, is an authentic nineteenth-century palace. This town was both the birthplace and residence of Agostino Coppola, grandfather of Francis Ford Coppola. In 2004, the renowned director purchased the palazzo with the vision of transforming it into a charming Italian boutique hotel, reconnecting him to his roots in Basilicata.

Alongside French designer Jacques Grange, the palace underwent a complete restoration by Francis Ford Coppola, driven by the desire to create a place "his children would want to revisit time and again." Palazzo Margherita has a singular atmosphere filled with memories immersed in a welcoming environment. Today, the palazzo not only serves as a testament to its historical significance but also stands as a living legacy, reflecting the shared vision and love of family.

EMBASSY Armchairs, 1982
Piero Pinto, inspired by the
Bonacina Historical Archive
pages 171, 174–75

CROCHET Sofas and armchairs, 1973
Mario Bonacina and Renzo Mongiardino
pages 172–73

II.
PATTERNS

Decorative Weaving Styles for a Natural Material

Rattan's natural qualities—pliancy and versatility—are the perfect metaphor for Bonacina's long-lasting resilience.

THE ART OF WEAVING RATTAN

Though wicker has been part of human civilization for thousands of years, woven rattan was introduced to the West at the height of the expansion of the Victorian empire. Marking the differences between common wicker and rattan is fundamental in understanding the quality of Bonacina—a distinction that Antonia Bonacina likens to comparing cotton to silk.

Over its 135 years, Bonacina has mastered the art of weaving rattan core into an array of different signature and made-to-order patterns. Their most classic weaves include *la treccia*, the classic braid; *la dama*, a checkered pattern; and *la finestrella*, an elaborate symmetry of open spaces, like many little windows in the weave. There are about six hundred species of rattan, but Bonacina uses only the best varieties of manila, manao, malacca, tohiti, and palasan sourced throughout the year from the Philippines, Indonesia, and Malaysia. Harvesting the vines—a painstaking process that must be done by hand—sustains the local communities while protecting the forest habitats where the vines thrive.

Rattan's natural qualities—pliancy and versatility—are the perfect metaphor for Bonacina's long-lasting resilience. When Giovanni Bonacina founded the company, woven furniture was all the rage in Europe and America, and in the early twentieth century, there were many makers in Italy and across Europe. Nearly all of them have since closed; the few that remain, except for Bonacina and one or two others, relocated their manufacturing to the Far East.

CROSS

With the addition of diagonal elements to the classic warp
(vertical components) and weft (horizontal components) structure,
the Cross strengthens the weave while becoming a decorative feature.

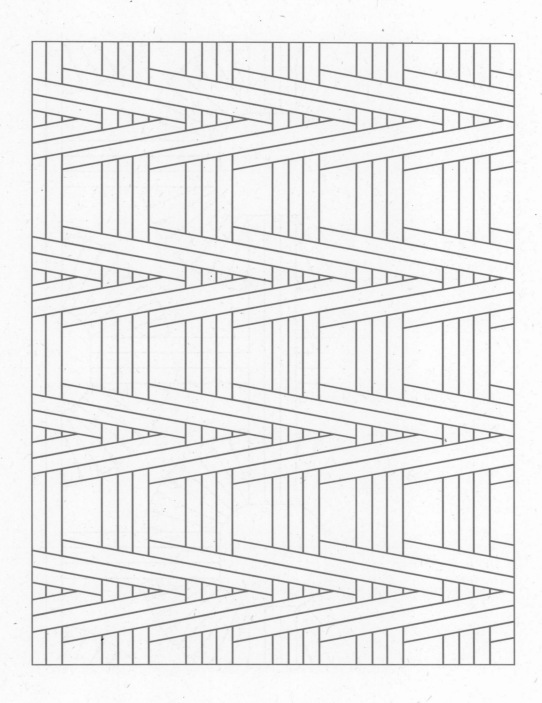

VIR

Shaped like overlapping chevrons, the Vir horizontally crosses over "free" strands of vertical rattan core—an essential technical element that strengthens and reinforces the weaving.

DONUT

The Donut pattern, often used for backrests, keeps the horizontal
and vertical rods properly spaced. Its round shape is both an
aesthetic choice that makes the design visually interesting and
a functional one, separating and holding the structure together.

DAMA

With a name that plays on the Italian words for *lady*
and *checkers*, the Dama decorative pattern is imbued
with feminine sophistication.

TRESS

Bonacina's only purely decorative feature, the Tress is applied to chairs at the end of production to finish its borders with a plait of three elements, each made of multiple strands of rattan core.

GRID

This very firm, double-woven pattern is often used for seats due
to its strength and resilience. The Grid can be woven with warp and
weft elements in the same color or, for a bolder result, in two colors.

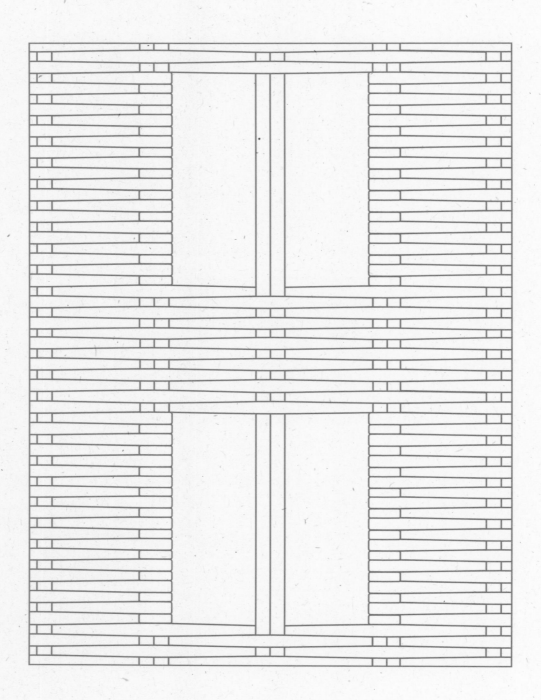

PEEPHOLE

Bestowing lightness on even a large-scale piece of furniture,
the Peephole pattern playfully mixes solids and voids to allow
glimpses through the rattan.

FISHBONE

Similar to the Grid pattern, the Fishbone creates a flexible
membrane of spaced double weaving whose warp and weft
can be modeled into various shapes.

DOPPIA

Symmetrical, clean-lined, and decorative, the Doppia (Italian for *double*) pattern also blocks the weave, making it extremely sturdy.

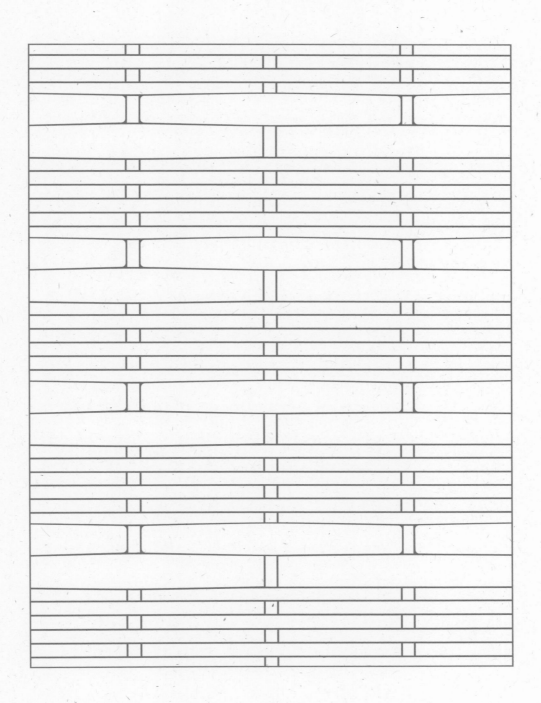

RULLO

Evoking the texture of a soft fabric, the Rullo (Italian for *roller*)
pattern lends a sense of coziness and welcome to a furniture design.

RADIANT

A decorative motif inspired by rays of sunlight, the Radiant
is perfectly offset by the open space surrounding it.

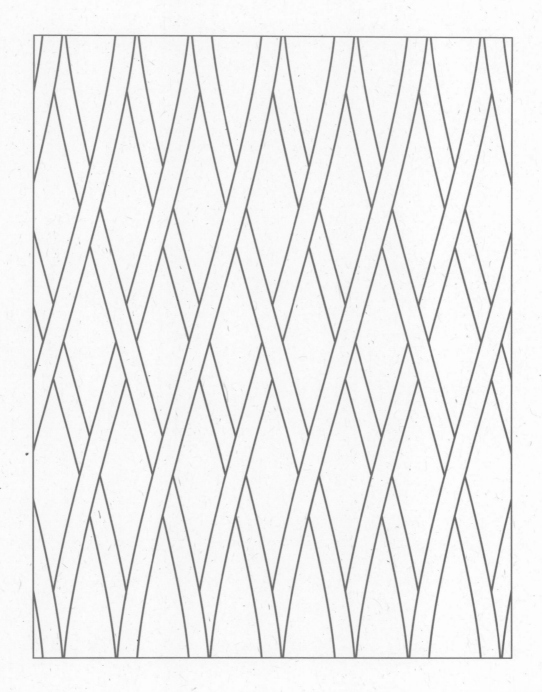

LOSANGA

In this advanced weaving technique, the warp and weft are
rotated and inclined. The Losanga (Italian for *lozenge*)
pattern has an intricate, slender, and transparent effect that
gives a feeling of lightness to the overall design.

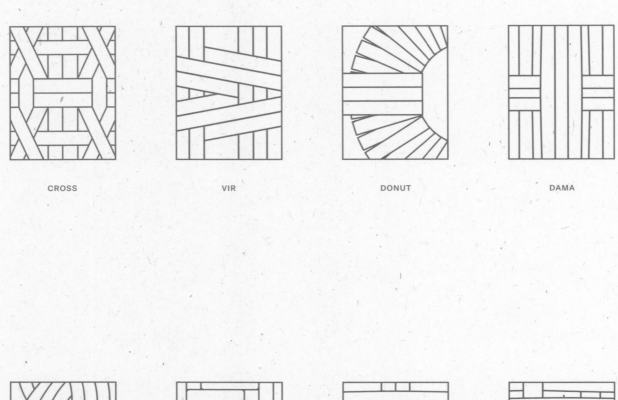

CROSS   VIR   DONUT   DAMA

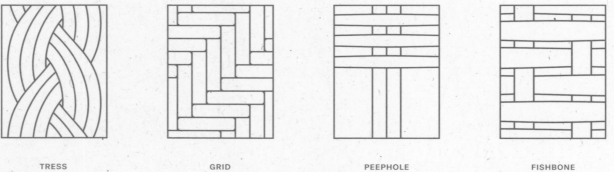

TRESS   GRID   PEEPHOLE   FISHBONE

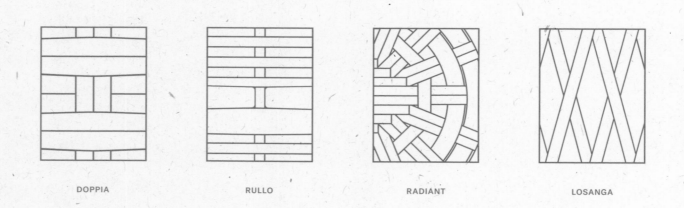

DOPPIA   RULLO   RADIANT   LOSANGA

III.
RATTAN

The Durable Climbing Palm from Southeast Asia

Rattan, a resilient climbing palm, thrives in the dense forests of the Far East, with high humidity that favors its growth. The vine is meticulously selected. With precision and care, a blade removes all its spines. The result is vibrant green cane with its outer skin. The vibrant green shade means that it has a higher level of sap.

The canes gracefully soak up the sunlight.

Boiling the rattan rids it of dirt and tiny parasites, making way for the intricate drawing process that breathes life into each cane. A mesmerizing array unfolds as clean rattan canes take on new forms—worked into various diameters or turned into flat threads, reminiscent of spaghetti.

The harvest is loaded into boats—or made to flow directly on the river—
destined for places where it will be further purified and refined.

The natural raw material undergoes a long journey on its way
to our laboratory in Italy.

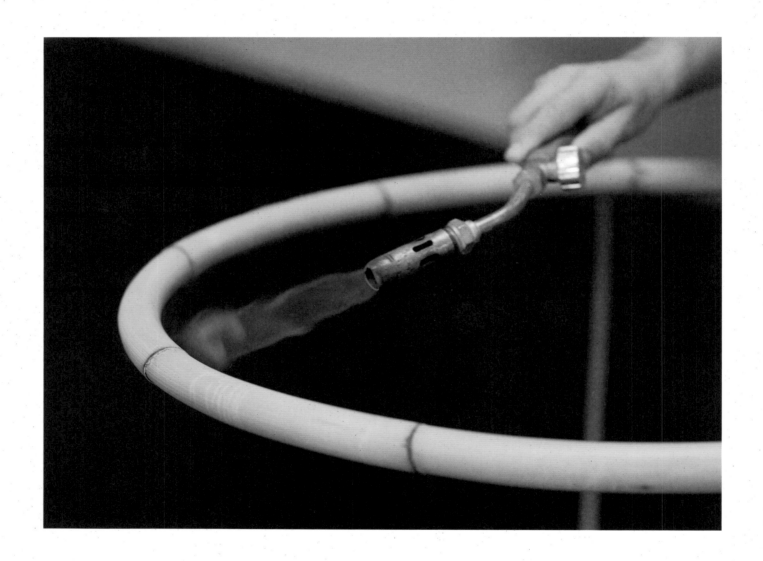

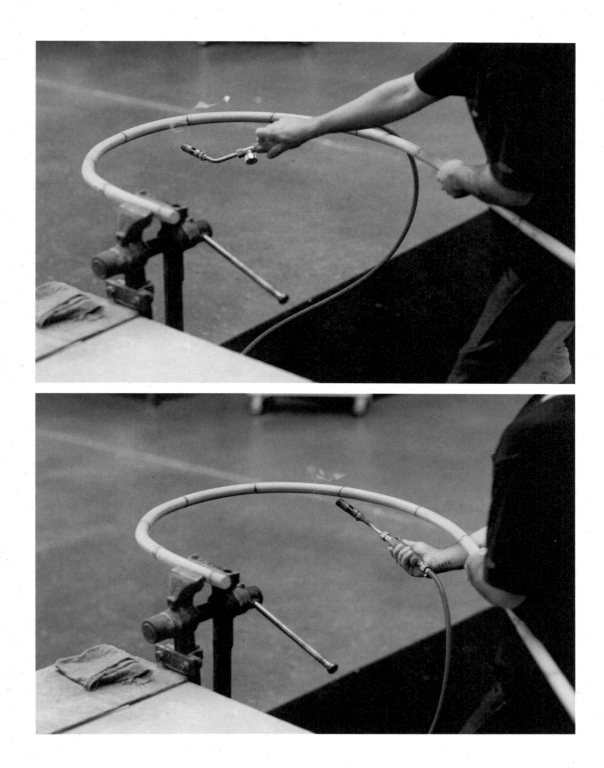

Bonacina craftspeople engage in a dance with fire, initiating the artful process of bending and shaping.

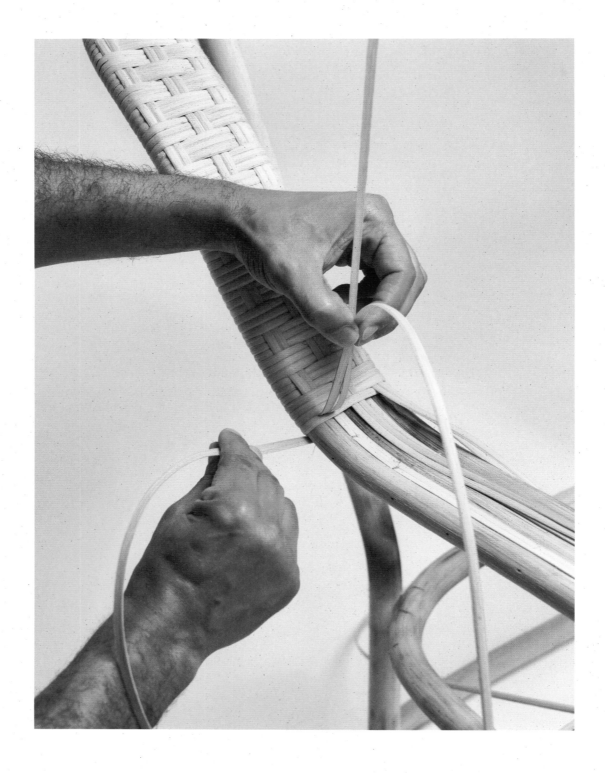

The Bonacina symphony: skilled artisans, akin to musicians, weave lower diameters of rattan core and flat rattan core threads into the piece's skeletal structure. Harmonious strands of tradition and innovation unite.

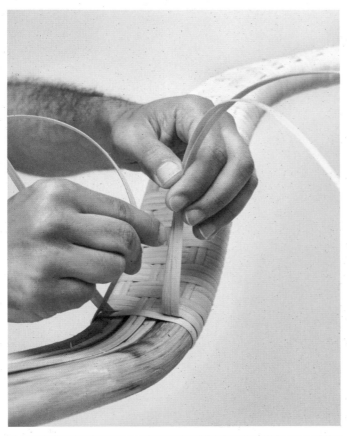

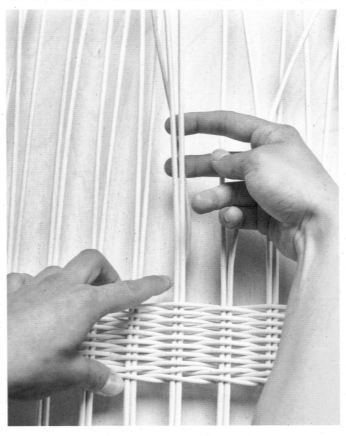

IV.
HISTORY

23.

15.

16.

24.

1889

2.

6.

17.

25.

3.

7.

11.

18.

26.

1.

4.

8.

12.

19.

5.

9.

13.

20.

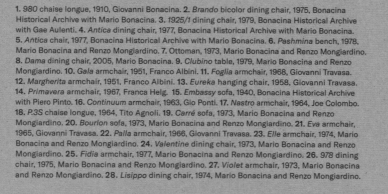

10.

14.

21.

27.

22.

28.

1. *980* chaise longue, 1910, Giovanni Bonacina. 2. *Brando* bicolor dining chair, 1975, Bonacina Historical Archive with Mario Bonacina. 3. *1925/1* dining chair, 1979, Bonacina Historical Archive with Gae Aulenti. 4. *Antica* dining chair, 1977, Bonacina Historical Archive with Mario Bonacina. 5. *Antica* chair, 1977, Bonacina Historical Archive with Mario Bonacina. 6. *Pashmina* bench, 1978, Mario Bonacina and Renzo Mongiardino. 7. Ottoman, 1973, Mario Bonacina and Renzo Mongiardino. 8. *Dama* dining chair, 2005, Mario Bonacina. 9. *Clubino* table, 1979, Mario Bonacina and Renzo Mongiardino. 10. *Gala* armchair, 1951, Franco Albini. 11. *Foglia* armchair, 1968, Giovanni Travasa. 12. *Margherita* armchair, 1951, Franco Albini. 13. *Eureka* hanging chair, 1958, Giovanni Travasa. 14. *Primavera* armchair, 1967, Franca Helg. 15. *Embassy* sofa, 1940, Bonacina Historical Archive with Piero Pinto. 16. *Continuum* armchair, 1963, Gio Ponti. 17. *Nastro* armchair, 1964, Joe Colombo. 18. *P.3S* chaise longue, 1964, Tito Agnoli. 19. *Carré* sofa, 1973, Mario Bonacina and Renzo Mongiardino. 20. *Bourlon* sofa, 1973, Mario Bonacina and Renzo Mongiardino. 21. *Eva* armchair, 1965, Giovanni Travasa. 22. *Palla* armchair, 1966, Giovanni Travasa. 23. *Elle* armchair, 1974, Mario Bonacina and Renzo Mongiardino. 24. *Valentine* dining chair, 1973, Mario Bonacina and Renzo Mongiardino. 25. *Fidia* armchair, 1977, Mario Bonacina and Renzo Mongiardino. 26. *978* dining chair, 1975, Mario Bonacina and Renzo Mongiardino. 27. *Violet* armchair, 1973, Mario Bonacina and Renzo Mongiardino. 28. *Lisippo* dining chair, 1974, Mario Bonacina and Renzo Mongiardino.

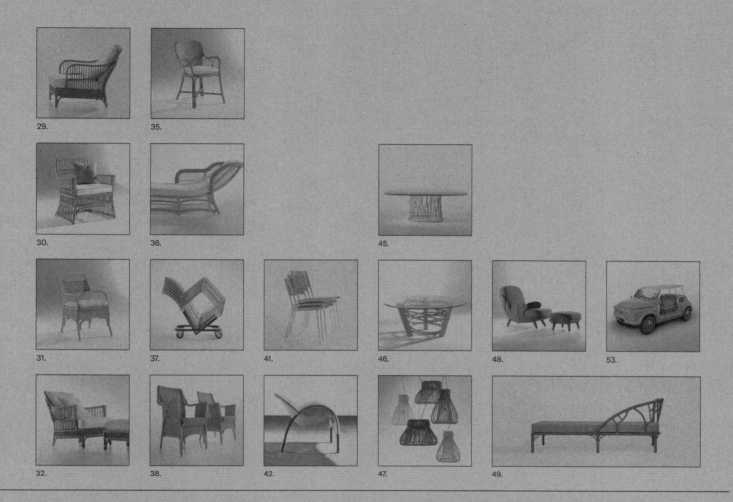

2024

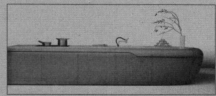

29. *Arpa* armchair, 1985, Mario Bonacina and Renzo Mongiardino. 30. *May Fair* armchair, 1977, Mario Bonacina and Renzo Mongiardino. 31. *Elle XS* dining chair, 1974, Mario Bonacina and Renzo Mongiardino. 32. *Talide* armchair and ottoman, 1975, Mario Bonacina and Renzo Mongiardino. 33. *Serra/F* armchair, 1981, Mario Bonacina and Renzo Mongiardino. 34. *Radiant* armchair, 1978, Mario Bonacina and Renzo Mongiardino. 35. *Martin* dining chair, circa 1980, Mario Bonacina and Renzo Mongiardino. 36. *1925/6* chaise longue, 1980, Mario Bonacina. 37. *S.21* chair, 1983, Tito Agnoli. 38. *MdO'* small armchair, 1984, Gae Aulenti. 39. *Enea* armchair, 1984, Mario Bonacina. 40. *1925/5* chair, 1980, Mario Bonacina. 41. *Miss B* chair, 1997, Tito Agnoli. 42. *Manta* armchair, 1998, D'Urbino Lomazzi. 43. *Flo* sofa, 1999, Francesco Bettoni. 44. *Ellipses* sofa, 2009, Giuseppe Viganò. 45. *Traccia* table, 2007, Francesco Bettoni. 46. *Union* table, 2007, Valerio Gaeti. 47. *Orbita* lamps, 2006, Tomoko Mizu. 48. *Siesta* armchair and pouf, 2010, Mattia Bonetti. 49. *Luca* chaise longue, 2023, Francis Sultana. 50. Kitchen, 2023, Ronen Joseph. 51. *Wild* chair, 2011, Piero Lissoni. 52. *Senzafine* coffee table, 2010, Mattia Bonetti. 53. Fiat 500 Spiaggina, 2023, Bonacina x Garage Italia.

215

Never forget that the universe is a single living organism possessed of one substance and one soul, holding all things suspended in a single consciousness and creating all things with a single purpose that they may work together, spinning and weaving and knotting whatever comes to pass.

MARCUS AURELIUS, *MEDITATIONS*, BOOK IV, 40

OPPOSITE The Bonacina family, pictured from top to bottom: Margherita Bonacina, product art director and co-owner, with her partner, Andrea Tinelli, plant manager. Elia Bonacina, president and chief executive officer, with his partner, Elena Daniela Lazar, sales executive. Mario and Antonia Bonacina, honorary president and vice president, respectively. Photographed at the family house, designed by architect Lorenzo Forges Davanzati.

FOLLOWING PAGES
The Bonacina living room with *Eva* armchairs, 1965, in malacca, design by Giovanni Travasa; *Senzafine* coffee table, 2010, design by Mattia Bonetti; and *Composit* shelves–chaises longues, 2014, design by Francesco Bettoni.

AN INTRODUCTION

Our world is in a different place from where it was in 1889 when Giovanni Bonacina, the progenitor of the Bonacina design dynasty, founded his rattan furniture company. At that time, Italy was settling into its new status as a united country, and the Belle Époque, with its burgeoning styles in architecture and interior design, was in full bloom. Within a few years, Giovanni's company, located among the hills and plains of Brianza, Lombardy, established itself as one of the most successful enterprises of its kind on the European continent.

Giovanni and his descendants ferried their company into the twentieth century, navigating it through two world wars and the turbulent years in their wake, and keeping course during numerous periods of fraught political and economic instability. When times were propitious, they invested in avant-garde design and, more recently, in state-of-the-art technologies. All the while, the focus has been on maintaining a balance between tradition and innovation. Now that the fourth generation of this entrepreneurial family is on board, the time is ripe to take a step back and observe the evolution of the Bonacina legacy.

Many tales have resurfaced during this process. Some are captured in the graininess of old photographs and in the yellowing pages of century-old Bonacina catalogs. Other stories have emerged from the collection of original prototypes, many of which were designed by some of the greatest Italian architects and designers of the twentieth century. Still others are woven into the pliant suppleness of the rattan material itself.

What brings these stories to life, what truly makes them shine, are the firsthand recollections of members of the present-day Bonacina family: Mario and Antonia and their two grown children, Elia and Margherita. Their memories, experiences, aspirations, and strategies create a narrative that weaves together the vision, talent, and resilience of four generations of men and women that have made the Bonacina brand what it is today. What emerges is a uniquely Italian experience. This is its story.

BONACINA TODAY

On any given day, Bonacina's headquarters, in the fertile and industrious region just south of the Italian Alps, offers a spectacle of high craftsmanship. Starring is the company's team of men and women who, through the dexterity of their hands, transform slender stems of rattan—a sustainable, eco-friendly material that grows abundantly in tropical forests—into sculptural design objects. The pieces are as graceful and versatile as they are resilient. The stage on which this spectacle takes place is the open space on the ground floor of the company's vast headquarters in Lurago d'Erba, a small industrial town just south of the romantic shores of Lake Como.

The Bonacina choreography begins each morning with a group of men who, using fire as their main tool, mold and bend the rattan canes with slow and sweeping gestures, plying each cane with the strength of their hands and the weight of their bodies. As they move to the ancient rhythms of their craft, a warm scent rises from the fire-heated canes, infusing the air with a fragrance reminiscent of sun-kissed hay or toasted bread. The curves and bends achieved in the process are then fixed by applying cold water with cloths. Other pieces are added until a streamlined structure or frame emerges from the craftsmen's hands and is passed on to those of the experienced weavers, mostly women, who sit nearby.

Then begins the second phase, just as mesmerizing and ritualistic as the first. After handpicking long thin strips of rattan core that have been soaked in fresh water, each weaver begins the process of entwining the threads into one of several elaborate Bonacina weaves. Depending on the size and design of the piece, this painstaking process takes one weaver anywhere between one and ten weeks to complete. The finished object is then taken to another area where it is stained, painted, or sealed and, when indicated, upholstered. Each phase is overseen by Mario Bonacina—Giovanni's grandson and a designer in his own right—and his daughter, Margherita. "At the core of Bonacina's designs," Mario explains, "is the pulsating heart of labor-intensive expertise that defines our brand."

THE COMPANY'S PRESENT CONFIGURATION

Before diving into the company's history, let us take a closer look at its present configuration. Mario joined the company in 1972, after graduating from the Industrial Design Institute of Florence, and eventually took the torch from his father, Giovanni's son Vittorio.

Throughout his long career, Mario has collaborated closely with influential Italian and international architects and designers, creating avant-garde designs and a more classical collection inspired by the work of his forebears. Antonia, Mario's wife, oversees special projects and liaises with foreign clients and the press; the couple have been working together since the early 1980s.

OPPOSITE A glimpse into the heart of Bonacina at the Lurago d'Erba headquarters. Pieces crafted with precision and care await their journey to locations worldwide.

Antonia's quest to share the Bonacina legacy inspired her to restore and classify the company's extensive archives: hundreds of pieces of furniture, home and travel accessories, and even children's toys housed in the Bonacina Museum. Inaugurated in February 2023, this museum retraces the company's evolution placing its postwar productions within the history of Italian twentieth-century design. The couple's daughter, Margherita, flanks Mario in overseeing the production of every design while their son, Elia, is chief executive officer. Together they uphold the Bonacina legacy of continuous inspiration, ever looking at it under a new light, a new color, or a new shape.

ELIA BONACINA, CHIEF EXECUTIVE OFFICER

Elia was twenty-two years old when he joined the company. Backed by his parents and sister, who gave him their full support, Elia made his first strategic move: acquiring Pierantonio Bonacina, a woven furniture company developed by another branch of the family and also based in Lurago d'Erba. "Entrusting the young, supporting their vision, and preserving the past by embracing the future, are the defining characteristics of this company's DNA," Elia said during an interview for this book. Pierantonio Bonacina's rich archive included iconic designs of the 1950s and '60s by star architects such as Joe Colombo, Gio Ponti, and Marco Zanuso, and a line of outdoor furniture made with state-of-the-art materials. The outdoor line of furniture added a new dimension to a company that, up until then, had relied solely on its handcrafted production of rattan furniture.

Elia's project to keep it all in the family would protect the legacy of both family endeavors. He decided to name the newly merged company *Bonacina*, honoring Giovanni as well as the talent and resourcefulness of the generations that succeeded him. Elia's strategies proved enormously successful: Since the merger, the company's yearly revenue has seen a twofold increase, and in 2022, *Forbes* included him in its list of the hundred most successful chief executive officers in Italy.

CURRENT PRODUCTION

Bonacina currently produces three collections of furniture and home accessories: *Grandi Maestri*, Décor, and Contemporary. *Grandi Maestri* (Great Masters) focuses on iconic pieces designed in collaboration with revolutionary Italian designers and architects since the 1950s: Tito Agnoli, Franco Albini, Joe Colombo, Franca Helg, Gio Ponti, and Marco Zanuso, to name a few. Their sometimes audacious choices fall within the Bonacina style thanks to the unmistakable, unifying nature of rattan. These pieces live well both in domestic environments and international museum collections, and are a sort of totemic fetish for aspiring designers and collectors today.

The Décor line is inspired by Mario Bonacina's longstanding collaboration with Renzo Mongiardino and his own creative incursions in the original Giovanni Bonacina catalog. Both as effortlessly pleasant and intricate as

BELOW Elia Bonacina graces the cover of *Forbes Small Giants*, December 2022.

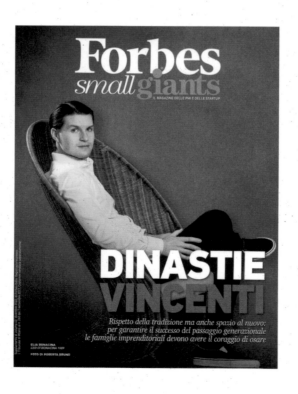

ABOVE LEFT *Primavera* armchair and prototype, 1967, design by Franca Helg; and *Gala* armchair, 1951, design by Franco Albini.

ABOVE RIGHT *Nastro* armchair and sofa, 1964, designs by Joe Colombo. Photographed at the Bonacina Museum.

the natural and botanical world, Décor furnishings represent the essence of Bonacina: a meeting of the most technical craftsmanship virtuosity and a taste for timeless Italian elegance. Décor also includes the outcome of the long-lasting collaborations between Bonacina and designers such as Gae Aulenti, Mattia Bonetti, and Francis Sultana.

Contemporary is the most innovative collection, blending the company's weaving know-how with high-tech materials resilient to ice, rain, and sunshine while never jeopardizing the brand's historical and artisanal values. For the Contemporary line, design masters such as Piero Lissoni and Marco Zanuso Jr. (a nephew of Marco Zanuso), together with new talents such as Francesco Bettoni, Franco Bizzozzero, and Giuseppe Viganò, experiment with materials and build on Bonacina's farsighted vision.

The company headquarters, which used to occupy an elegant nineteenth-century compound near the center of Lurago d'Erba, was relocated in July 2021 to an industrial warehouse on the outskirts of town. The sixty-five-thousand square feet include the vast ground floor where the entire cycle of the Bonacina handcrafted production takes place. The upper floor is an efficiently designed space that hosts the family and its collaborators.

FOUNDER GIOVANNI BONACINA AND THE BELLE ÉPOQUE

The story of Bonacina is a time-honed narrative with a youthful heart. It all started in the mid-1880s, during Europe's grand Belle Époque, when Giovanni Bonacina, a teenager born and bred in Lurago d'Erba, had a brilliant intuition. By the 1880s, the industrial revolution had produced a wealthy Italian bourgeoisie that built houses and mansions and looked to England, and its gilded Victorian age, for new styles of living. Woven furniture had made its way from Asia to Great Britain's gardens, its salons, and even its royal abodes. From there, it trickled southward and eastward, infusing a breezy elegance into the homes and gardens of Europe. Giovanni had an inkling that Italy's master weavers could produce exceptional rattan furniture that would capture this new audience.

At sixteen, Giovanni enrolled in a school in Milan that provided superb vocational training. Since 1881, when Milan hosted the International Exposition, an extraordinary event that attracted more than a million visitors, the city had established itself as the cultural and industrial capital of Italy. Studying there opened Giovanni's eyes to emerging styles of interior decoration where woven furniture—his first love—played a growing part. He had discovered the beauty and versatility of rattan through some Dutch merchants, who were importing it from Indonesia.

As soon as his studies were completed, Giovanni returned to his hometown, determined to invest in the weaving traditions of the local *canestrai*, who for generations had been transforming reeds, grasses, and willows that grew along the border of the Po River into all kinds of basketry. His mission was to apply that know-how to a line of luxury furniture and home accessories using rattan instead of the humble natural fibers they were used to.

PRECEDING PAGES More than a thousand prototypes are meticulously preserved at the Bonacina Historical Archive.

OPPOSITE *1925/5 Out* outdoor dining chairs, in a spectrum of colors.

Giovanni was barely twenty years old when, in 1889, he opened the doors of his own company, Giovanni Bonacina.

In the peaceful and expansive years that followed, the Italian bourgeoisie were building mountain lodges, country mansions, and seaside retreats. Influenced by Britain's horticultural imports, Europeans began planting palm trees and other exotic species in their gardens, which they furnished as extensions of their interiors.

In a race to meet the growing demands of a clientele that included members of the great industrial families of the time, such as the Florios in Sicily, the Agnellis in Piedmont, and the Visconti di Modrone in Emilia Romagna, Bonacina expanded its production. Within a handful of years, it went from employing roughly five specialized workers to more than one hundred. Its designs were presented at the most important international exhibitions and won many prizes, including gold medals at the 1909 Imperial International Exhibition in London, the 1909 Exposition Internationale d'Economie Domestique in Paris, and the 1910 Esposizione di Prodotti Agricoli Industriali di Roma.

MARGHERITA DI SAVOIA AND THE END OF THE BELLE ÉPOQUE

There is a photograph in the Bonacina Historical Archive that bears witness to the high regard and prestigious clientele the company had reached by the end of the Belle Époque. It is a black-and-white portrait of Margherita di Savoia, Italy's Queen Mother, sitting on a finely woven Bonacina armchair

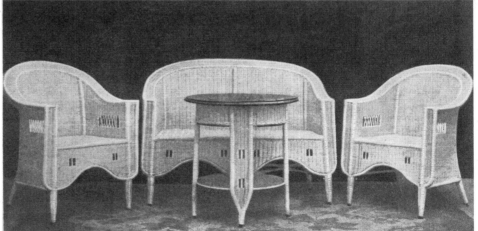

ABOVE Portrait of Giovanni
Bonacina, late 1950s.

TOP RIGHT AND RIGHT
In the catalog published by
Giovanni Bonacina in the early
twentieth century, it is possible
to see products that are still in
production, such as pieces from the
Brando, *Vittoria*, and *Antica* lines.

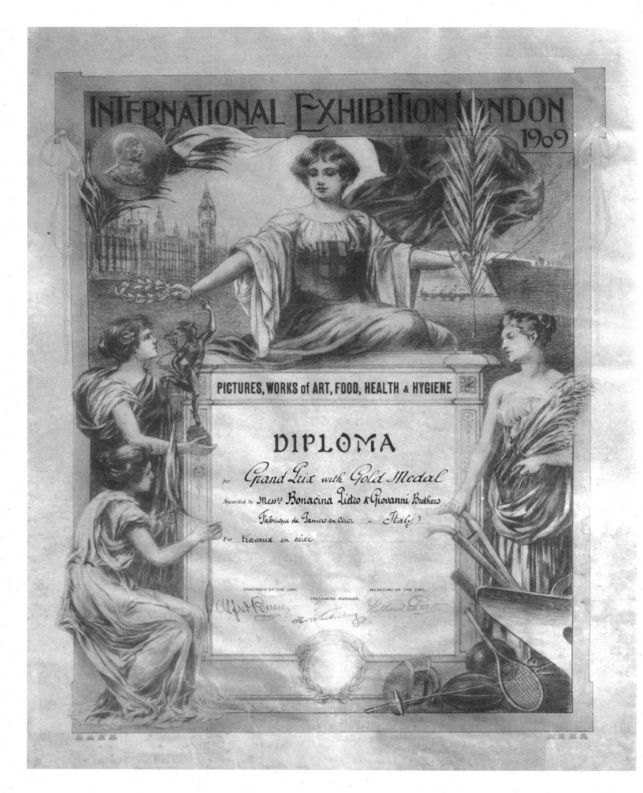

OPPOSITE The designs of
Giovanni Bonacina were presented
at the most important international
exhibitions and won many prizes,
including gold medals at the 1909
International Exhibition in London,
the 1909 Exposition Internationale
d'Economie Domestique in
Paris, and the 1910 Esposizione
di Prodotti Agricoli Industriali di
Roma. Bonacina Historical Archive.

RIGHT Gold medals from
international exhibitions in Paris
(1909), Rome (1910), and London
(1909). Bonacina Historical Archive.

BELOW Export price list from
1925 that includes sales and
payment conditions, as well as
specific export prices, indicating
how often the company traded
with foreign countries from
the time of the firm's founding.
Bonacina Historical Archive.

IMPORTANTE:

Per un salotto a 6 pezzi si intendono i seguenti :
2 Poltrone - 2 Sedie - 1 Divano - 1 Tavolo.

Per un salotto a 4 pezzi si intendono i seguenti :
2 Poltrone - 1 Divano - 1 Tavolo.

Condizioni Generali di Vendita

1. - La merce viaggia a rischio e pericolo del Committente anche se venduta franco destino ;
2. - Non rispondo dei danni od ammanchi causati dagli enti che effettuano il trasporto, ai quali deve essere rivolto il reclamo dal Committente ;
3. - Le epoche di Consegna sono rispettate solo se da me confermate per iscritto, salvo cause di forza maggiore, e le ritengo adempiute all'atto della spedizione ;
4. - Gli imballi verranno fatturati al costo e non li ricevo di ritorno. Per vagone completo, imballo gratis.

PAGAMENTI:

Sono validi solo se fatti al mio domicilio entro i 30 giorni dal ricevimento della merce, trascorso i quali verrà emessa senza alcun avviso tratta con spese. - Per ditte conosciute condizioni speciali.

Per qualunque controversia eleggo a competenza il foro di Como.

GIOVANNI BONACINA

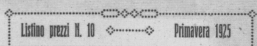

Listino prezzi N. 10 ◇———◇ Primavera 1925

GIOVANNI BONACINA

(Como)   LURAGO D'ERBA   (Italia)

PREMIATA FABBRICA

DI

MOBILI e CESTERIE in VIMINI, GIUNCO

MIDOLLO e MALACCA

◠◡

ESPORTAZIONE

Sconto _____ % Aumento _____ %

in the open loggia of her villa in Bordighera, on the rocky coastline of Liguria. She is in her mid-sixties. Her curly white hair is combed back, and she is wearing a long black dress in mourning for her husband, King Umberto I, who had been murdered in Monza in 1900.

Villa Regina Margherita di Savoia sits high on a hill, with stunning views of the sea. Commissioned from architect Luigi Broggi in 1914, the four-story building, which took just two years to complete, pays tribute to Baroque architecture but had all the modern comforts, including an elevator and an electrified bell system in every bedroom. Though the interiors were opulently furnished, the area in which the Queen Mother spent most of her time reading and tending to her potted plants was the loggia. It was here, on Bonacina furniture, that she and her inner circle of family and friends, including members of various European royal families and a select group of poets and artists, would gather daily.

The Queen Mother's posture in the photograph, sitting sideways on the armchair looking straight into the camera, suggests an intimate informality. Scattered on the sunny loggia are a handful of Bonacina chairs in the same style as the armchair on which she is sitting: a rounded back and an elaborate pattern of diagonal stripes woven on the seats. A pile of books rests on a matching Bonacina table.

BONACINA DURING THE WAR YEARS

During the war years, Giovanni adapted the company to the circumstances. Virtually overnight, the craftspeople he employed went from creating furniture for homes and gardens to producing a line of basketry for the Italian army. Some items were designed to be mounted on mules for the transportation of arms and munitions. Other pieces, such as wicker-and-leather trunks, were used by alpine soldiers to transport food and carrier pigeons, essential for communication from the frontlines.

GIOVANNI'S TREASURED 1925 COLLECTION

Once the turbulence receded, the lessons learned did not get shelved. A rare and precious object in the Bonacina Historical Archive bears testimony to this: a booklet with a soft, pastel-blue cover, containing a series of black-and-white photographs illustrating the company's main designs between 1920 and 1925, published by Giovanni in the aftermath of the First World War. He must have realized that if there was anything to be learned from the wreckage, it was that everything can be destroyed, but nothing is lost forever.

Giovanni's company flourished during the interwar years. Private patrons and hotels relied on Bonacina for their increasingly ambitious projects. Count Giuseppe Visconti, for example, commissioned many pieces for his family estate in Grazzano Visconti, near Piacenza. Clara Agnelli, the wife of Fiat founder Senatore Giovanni Agnelli, bought stacks

OPPOSITE Pieces from the early 1900s, safeguarded in the Bonacina Historical Archive.

FOLLOWING PAGES
The Bonacina Museum is divided into four distinct sections, each representing a period of the brand's generational evolution.

1889

FON
DAZIO
NE
FOUN
D

Giovanni Bonacina, Diego Carnelutti

Creatore di tradizione

Giovanni Bonacina: dedizione, visione e un pizzico di audacia

The Tradition Maker

Giovanni Bonacina: dedication, vision, and a touch of audacity

Un luogo speciale

La vicinanza con Milano, il territorio dell'Impero Austro ungarico e il Lago di Como rende la Brianza lo scenario perfetto

A very special place

The proximity to Milan, to the territory of the Austro-Hungarian Empire and to Como Lake unites Brianza the perfect scenario

Un materiale esotico

Un materiale proveniente dal Sud-Est asiatico dotato di flessibilità, malleabilità e durevolezza

A material from afar

A material coming from Southeast Asia with flexibility, malleability and durability

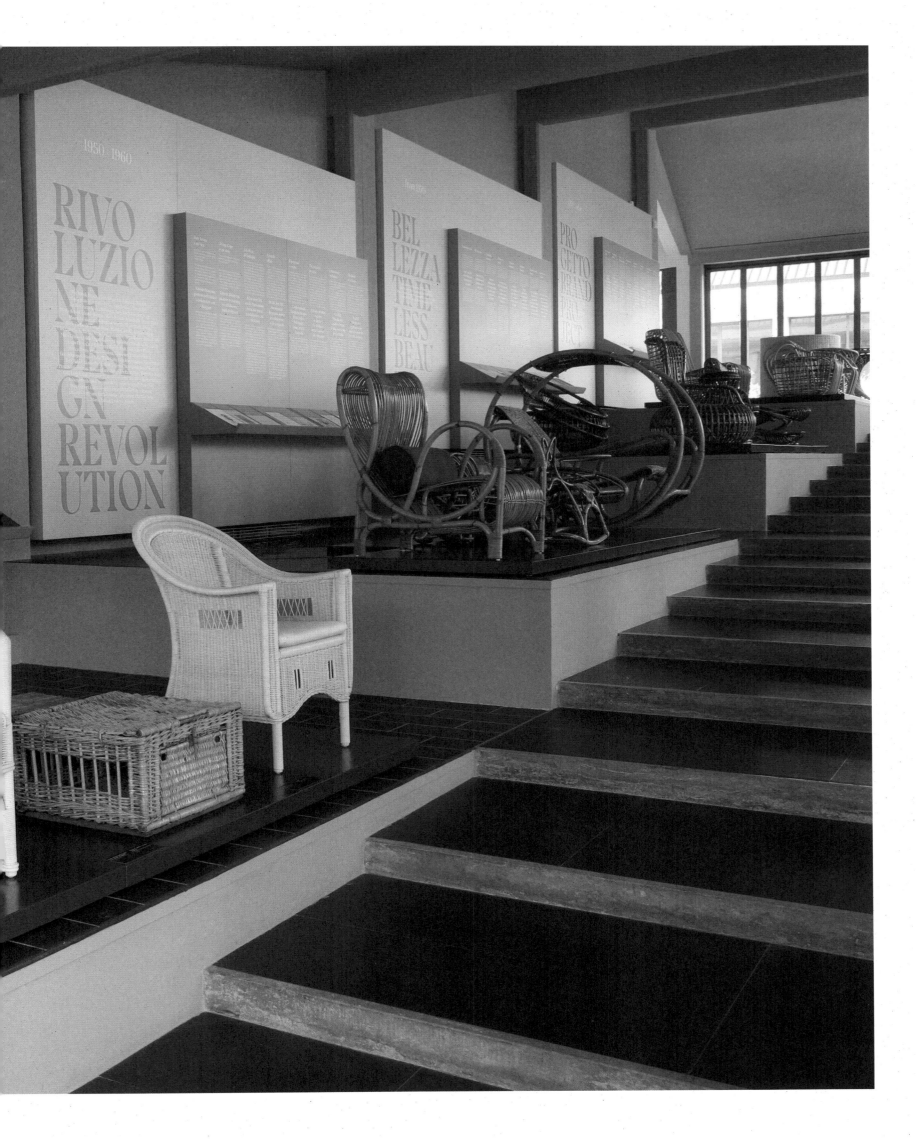

of chairs and tables to furnish the garden and open loggia of their family home in Villar Perosa, the one-time royal hunting lodge designed by architect Juvarra. Black-and-white photographs from the 1930s capture the elegance and poise that reigned around the Bonacina lounges and tables on the grounds of Hotel Villa d'Este, the Renaissance villa on the shores of Lake Como.

The reverence with which the current Bonacina family members consult Giovanni's 1925 catalog, turning each page with tender care, is indicative of how they treasure the family legacy. The booklet continues to be a huge source of inspiration for Mario and for the many architects and designers who have consulted it.

TRAVEL

In virtue of the innate lightness of rattan—a chair can weigh under five pounds—Bonacina's pieces became indispensable travel accessories. At the end of the nineteenth century, when flying hot-air balloons became a fashionable sport among the very wealthy, the company produced balloon baskets using the more resilient rattan. Around that time, a funicular in Naples was furnished with Bonacina furniture, as were some first-class train wagons. Bonacina's made-to-measure rattan trunks and picnic baskets became popular accessories for motor-car excursions, and 1920s photographs reveal the interiors of an airship, one of the very first built for commercial travel: Giovanni furnished it with woven rattan chairs fixed to the floor using metal rods.

Bonacina continues to lend its services to the travel industry. The brand furnishes hotels, as we have seen, motorboats, cruise boats, yachts, and private jets. On the occasion of a 1994 benefit for AIDS research Mario Bonacina and Mario Cananzi designed a woven rattan bicycle for an auction held at the Triennale Design Museum Milan.

THE YEARS OF THE DESIGN REVOLUTION: VITTORIO AND CARLA BONACINA

Once peace was declared after the Second World War, Milan got its act together very quickly by transforming the devastation of the war years into an opportunity to experiment with new ideas in architecture and design. It was an optimistic period, and a new wave of young creative professionals wanted to forget the war and the harsh years that led up to it.

One symbol of this resurgence was La Rinascente, the popular department store located in an elaborate nineteenth-century building that had been badly damaged during the 1943 Allied air raids. A stone's throw from the Duomo, it was rebuilt from scratch in a handful of years by architect Ferdinando Reggiori. The new La Rinascente, inaugurated in time for the 1950 Christmas season, was hailed in the press. The interiors were just as slick and avant-garde as the exteriors. They had been designed by Carlo Pagani, a young

ABOVE *980* adjustable chaise longue, 1910, design by Giovanni Bonacina. With its visionary design, it remains an icon.

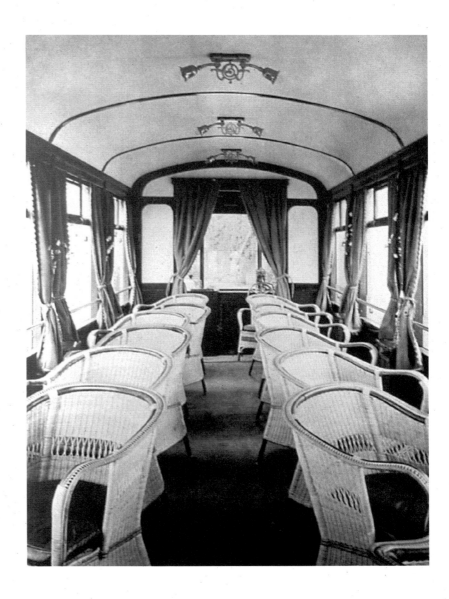

RIGHT AND BELOW Train and funicular interiors from the early twentieth century.

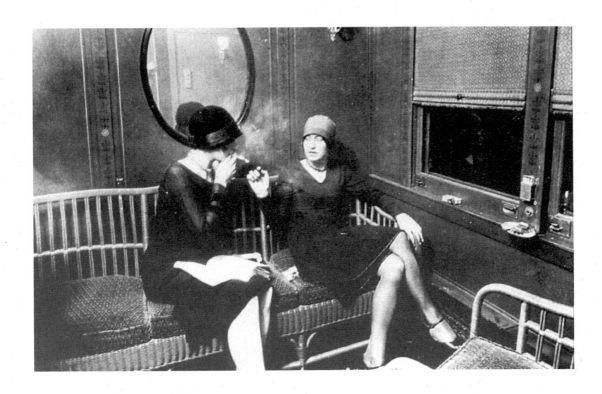

architect who had spent the war years editing *Domus*, the influential periodical on design and architecture founded in 1928 by Pagani's friend and mentor Gio Ponti. As a center of design, La Rinascente promoted architects such as Franco Albini, Liisi Beckmann, and Franca Helg, all of whom eventually approached Bonacina with their ideas for woven furniture and home accessories.

Back in Lurago d'Erba, a private but no less consequential renaissance was taking place. It all began in 1951, the year Giovanni Bonacina nominated his son Vittorio as his successor. A cultivated man with a passion for history, Vittorio had been working side by side with his father for years. His strong work ethic, combined with an experimental frame of mind, gave him the tools to lead the company's transition from a successful rattan furniture enterprise into something far more ambitious: an innovative company that would bring together the best minds and talents of postwar architecture and design with the most qualified craftsmanship Vittorio could muster. "My father-in-law's poetic and artistic sensibility, together with his innate curiosity," notes Antonia Bonacina, "led him to forge relationships, which at times turned into friendships, with some of the most avant-garde architects and designers of that period." Carefully managing the family business, Carla, Vittorio's wife, a determined and dedicated woman, played a fundamental role in the development of the company during those years.

FRANCO ALBINI

One of Vittorio's first and perhaps most defining collaborations was with Franco Albini, a leading figure of Rationalism and one of the undisputed fathers of industrial design in Italy. Albini's ethos, shared by Vittorio, revolved around an oxymoron: to curb the excesses of traditional Italian artisanship, which had flourished during the Belle Époque, to meet the new stylistic criteria of avant-garde and internationalist design. The immediate result of the Albini–Bonacina collaboration was two armchairs. The first was named *Margherita*, after the daisy. Its solid, curvaceous malacca rattan structure, supporting a fine weave of Indian cane, is the very first example in Italian design of an armchair whose legs have been replaced by a circular base. *Margherita* went on to win the Gold Medal at Milan's IX Triennale. The second outcome of Vittorio and Franco's collaboration was the *Gala*, a malleable and generously comfortable armchair defined by its lightweight and transparent structure in rattan and Indian canze. Featured in several road movies, including Alberto Sordi's iconic Amore mio aiutami (*Help Me, My Love*, 1962), the *Margherita* was burnished in the collective imagination as another Bonacina mid-twentieth-century classic. *Gala* and *Margherita* armchairs are present in the permanent design collections of the Vitra Design Museum in Weil am Rhein, Germany, and at the Triennale Design Museum Milan.

WOMEN IN DESIGN

The design avant-garde of 1950s Milan was a creative arena. In 1951, the same time the *Margherita* and the *Gala* armchairs were released, Franca Helg, one of Italy's first successful female architects, joined Franco Albini's studio. A devotee of Rationalism and industrial design, Helg, the grande dame of Italian architecture, was keen to experiment with handcrafted materials. Albini and Helg had worked together for nearly three decades when she approached Bonacina in the 1960s with ideas for woven rattan furniture. Years later, looking at her drawings, Mario was surprised by how different her delicate yet rigorous aesthetic was from Albini's more Rationalist style. After working side by side with Bonacina's artisans in order to deeply understand how to work with rattan, Helg designed tables and clothes hangers for the company. But it was her *Primavera* armchair, produced in 1967, that made history. This tall-backed, armless chair combines the controlled rigor of a solid structure with the delicacy of a complex trellised weave. Helg is recognized as one of the protagonists of modern Italian design, and her classic creations are still part of Bonacina's collection today, as well as represented in the permanent design collections of the Philadelphia Museum of Art and the Triennale Design Museum Milan.

RIGHT Part of the *Grandi Maestri* collection of iconic pieces, from left to right: *Primavera* armchair, 1967, design by Franca Helg; and *Gala* and *Margherita* armchairs, 1951, designs by Franco Albini. Photographed at the Bonacina Museum.

Antonia Bonacina, who spent years restoring and classifying the company archive, emphasizes the fascinating work of female designers in the collection. Among these, we can mention Gae Aulenti, Liisi Beckmann, Mary Block, Anna Buffa, Gilda D'Agaro, Marta Latis, Anna Monti (Studio Monti GPA), Rosanna Monzini, Luisa Parisi, and Carla Venosta, all deserving of recognition for their dedication to design culture and multiple prestigious awards.

Though Aulenti went on to become one of the greatest Italian architects of the last fifty years, most women who graduated in architecture in the 1950s tended to be industrial designers. Raffaella Crespi was one of them. Crespi, professor of Architecture Technology and Industrial Design at Politecnico di Milano, was among the founders of ADI (Association for Industrial Design) and the first woman to hold the position of president of the Order of Architects of Milan. The most memorable of her designs for Bonacina, and perhaps the most lighthearted, was *Chiave di Violino* (Treble Clef), a sinuous armchair designed in 1957 and rewarded with the esteemed Compasso d'Oro prize in the same year.

Another Crespi model, *Disco Volante* (Flying Saucer), produced in 1959, is a child's pedal car in the elliptical shape of a woven rattan spaceship. Like a spiderweb—beautiful, light, and dynamic—it paved the way for a collection of products made from woven rattan specifically for children: rocking horses, elephants, turtles, and other animals that were designed with great enthusiasm and with the same care and attention as the furniture. Children in the postwar era had just a handful of toys, and those from Bonacina were extremely well made of natural materials. In that cultural moment, Antonia reflects, the lesson was that children had to look after their toys and if they broke, someone would repair them. Though the company no longer makes children's toys, its products have always been designed and crafted to stand the test of time, and Bonacina retains a "reusable" spirit by offering a restoration service.

MARIO BONACINA: A SENSITIVE SOUL AND TALENTED DESIGNER

In the early 1970s, when the taste for synthetic materials and industrially made furnishings flooded the market, Bonacina's creativity and resilience were again put to the test. Although the modernist revolution that Vittorio had started in the 1950s gained momentum in the 1960s, it had now come to a near standstill. That was the predicament Mario Bonacina faced in 1972, when he graduated from design school and joined the company, tasked with ferrying the company toward new horizons.

An important opportunity arose in 1973 when Renzo Mongiardino, the master of set design and interior decoration—whose client list included the Agnellis, the Rothschilds, the Queen of the Netherlands, and Audrey Hepburn—was commissioned by Baron Hans Heinrich Thyssen-Bornemisza to redecorate La Favorita, the monumental seventeenth-century villa and art museum in Castagnola, on the shores of Lake Lugano. The architect—referred to as the Maestro—had worked with Vittorio Bonacina on set designs

LEFT *Disco Volante* (Flying Saucer) toy spaceship, 1959, design by Raffaella Crespi. The design won a Compasso d'Oro prize.

BELOW *501* chair, 1958, design by Raffaella Crespi.

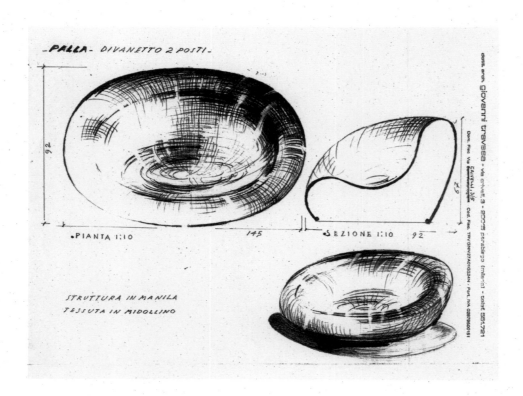

LEFT Sketches for the *Palla* two-seater sofa, 1966, design by Giovanni Travasa. Bonacina Historical Archive.

OPPOSITE Organic shapes from the *Grandi Maestri* collection, from left to right: *Foglia* armchair, 1968; *Eva* armchair, 1965; *Eureka* armchair, 1958; and *Palla* armchair, 1966; designs by Giovanni Travasa. Photographed at the Bonacina Museum.

BELOW Preparatory drawings by Giovanni Travasa, 1960s, for the *Eva* and *Foglia* armchairs. Bonacina Historical Archive.

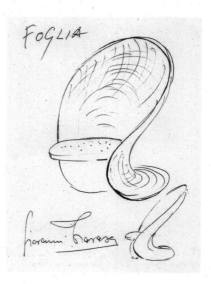

for Franco Zeffirelli, Peter Hall, and Giancarlo Menotti. He wanted to lighten up La Favorita's interiors and gardens with woven furnishings, so he approached Bonacina. "Before commissioning us for the Thyssen-Bornemisza project," Mario recalls, "Mongiardino needed to gauge my abilities."

Inspired by Giovanni's 1925 catalog, the architect made a technical drawing of a chaise longue and asked Mario to reproduce it. Back in Lurago d'Erba, the young designer, with all the nerve of his twenty-six years, made several changes to the original. When Mongiardino saw the finished product, he was delighted. That moment sealed the creative relationship between the famous architect and the young designer, one that would last forever. "The Maestro didn't make any more drawings for us — it wasn't necessary. He simply made a few very quick sketches, which I then elaborated on and turned into finished products.

"We would meet every Tuesday morning at his home studio in Milan at nine-thirty sharp," Mario recalls. The apartment, he explains, was richly decorated while his studio, filled with books, drawings, tiles, fabric samples, and other decorative accessories, exuded a work-in-progress atmosphere that was simpler and far more efficient. "He would invariably appear at our meetings wearing an elegant burgundy-red silk dressing gown over his pajamas," Mario adds fondly. "We would spend those morning meetings reinventing new pieces inspired by the old catalog. I sketched while he talked. Then I would return to our headquarters to complete the designs and oversee their creation. Mongiardino trusted me and I learned so much in the process."

Mario, a talented designer in his own right, began producing his own line of woven furniture, sometimes inspired by Rationalist design. "Mongiardino told me that, when he was young, he had been a devoted rationalist," Mario recalls. "But then, after a heated discussion with Gio Ponti, one of his professors at the Milano Politecnico, where Mongiardino graduated in 1942, he preferred decorative arts over rationalism." For many years, every piece designed by Mario with Mongiardino was destined exclusively for the architect's clients. In the early 1990s, it was Antonia who gathered together some of those design drawings and created the first Décor catalog.

GAE AULENTI AND THE MUSÉE D'ORSAY

The late 1980s were marked by another extraordinary commission, from Gae Aulenti. Having just won the project to transform the Gare d'Orsay in Paris into a museum, the Milanese architect asked Mario to create a prototype for a stackable chair to propose as seating for the museum's Impressionist galleries, the Café de l'Ours, and the restaurant.

"It was highly unlikely that we would get the commission," says Mario. "François Mitterand, the French president, had told Gae that, although he was pleased she had won the commission, it was de rigueur that all furniture and interiors be made in France." That prototype was born during a long phone call. "While Aulenti was talking, I was taking notes." Gae wanted to respect the architectural style of the Gare d'Orsay, which was built in 1900.

OPPOSITE Sketches by Mario Bonacina, from top to bottom: *1925/5* dining chair, 1980; *Carson* console, 2021; and *1925/6* chaise longue, 1980. All designs by Mario Bonacina. The *1925/5* chair is one of the brand's most popular designs. The *Carson* console are one of Mario's latest creations, while the *1925/6* chaise longue represents a timeless design from the 1980s.

ABOVE Furniture from a 1970s Bonacina catalog depicts that decade's characteristic use of wide-diameter canes. Both designs by Mario Bonacina.

RIGHT Table with wooden structure covered in bamboo plywood, 1974, design by Mario Bonacina.

VITTORIO BONACINA   LURAGO D'ERBA-COMO-ITALIA

VITTORIO BONACINA LURAGO D'ERBA COMO ITALIA

OPPOSITE Preparatory drawings, 1957, by Lorenzo Forges Davanzati of the *647* chair and *648* dining chair. Bonacina Historical Archive.

RIGHT *956* table, 1977, design by Lorenzo Forges Davanzati.

248

The starting point, once again, was the 1925 catalog and its Belle Époque designs. "During that first phone call, Aulenti mentioned a room designed by Le Corbusier where there was a rattan chair. I knew which one she was referring to," says Mario Bonacina. "She liked it because it wouldn't obstruct the view. 'It must be very lightweight, with a delicate weave,' she told me." By the end of the phone call, the sketch was done.

The prototype was passed on to several French furniture companies, but the result didn't meet the architect's expectations: Bonacina got the commission. Aulenti wanted the weaves to have hints of pastel color and handed Mario two bars of soap, one yellow and one pale blue, asking him to replicate them. In total, Bonacina produced eight hundred chairs for the Museé d'Orsay. "It was an extraordinary feat," recalls Mario, considering the delivery time required, "but we managed to deliver them in time for the grand opening."

"Before we started working together," Mario concludes, "I had been a little anxious. Gae Aulenti, I'd been told, could be imperious. The reality was quite different. She was an incredibly gracious person to work with."

Thanks to the success of that first commission, Mario Bonacina went on to create numerous other pieces for Gae Aulenti, many of which she used to furnish the houses she designed for Marella Agnelli in Saint Moritz and Marrakech. Several of Gae Aulenti's designs remain in the Bonacina catalog.

MAESTRO FEDERICO FORQUET AND THE AGNELLIS

Mario Bonacina's first commission for one of Gianni and Marella Agnelli's houses occurred in the early 1970s. The couple had settled on a large apartment on the fifth floor of a late nineteenth-century palace, one of the tallest residential buildings in Rome. "Mongiardino conceived a project that was a bit too nostalgic for Gianni's tastes," Forquet recalls. Then, Philip Johnson proposed a too futuristic project. Marella and Gianni turned to Ward Bennett, a self-taught New York designer who loved the arts and had studied briefly under Constantin Brancusi in prewar Paris. The work on the house took a couple of years.

Travertine stone—a tribute to Rome's imperial architecture—lined the entrance, from floor to ceiling. To warm up the living room, defined by high ceilings and soaring views over the city, Marella commissioned Mario Bonacina to make two elegantly woven daybeds. In the early 1980s, Marella asked Forquet to help her freshen up the apartment. Inspired by Mario's daybeds, they expanded on the Bonacina woven furniture theme by adding woven rattan sofas, chairs, and tables in nearly every room. Those two Bonacina daybeds, in other words, marked the beginning of a fruitful collaboration with Marella Agnelli that would last a lifetime.

PAST / PRESENT

If it is true that destiny, as Rainer Maria Rilke once wrote, is a wonderful wide tapestry in which every thread, guided by an unspeakably tender hand,

ABOVE Folder containing the contract for the commission of works for the Musée d'Orsay project and preparatory drawings for the *MdO'* armchairs with Gae Aulenti in 1984. Bonacina Historical Archive.

OPPOSITE TOP Museé d'Orsay restaurant with the *MdO'* armchairs, 1984, design by Gae Aulenti. Eight hundred chairs were delivered by Bonacina in the autumn of 1986 for the November inauguration, for which President François Mitterrand was present. Bonacina Historical Archive.

OPPOSITE FAR LEFT Preparatory drawing by Mario Bonacina for the *MdO'* armchair.

OPPOSITE NEAR LEFT *MdO'* armchair, 1984, design by Gae Aulenti.

is placed beside another thread, and then held and carried by a hundred others, then weaving itself is an art that captures the essence of time, giving form to its elusive rhythms. This poetic analogy helps us understand why Bonacina's history and the innovations it has achieved along the way are inextricably linked.

The living link between Bonacina's past and present is Mario. He embodies the continuity between experience and innovation. Born in 1947, Mario was twenty-five years old when he entered the business. His childhood memories are filled with the bustling activities in the company's headquarters, which at the time were located next to the family home. "My grandfather Giovanni and my father Vittorio worked side by side for years," he recalls. "They taught me a fundamental lesson: to survive in an evolving world, one had to be open to new ideas." Throughout a career spanning more than five decades, Mario has worked with some of the greatest talents of his time. His role has been twofold: finding technical solutions to complex designs, and remaining true to Bonacina's historic legacy. It was Mario's idea to honor the past through the Iconic line of twentieth-century designs. He also created his own successful line of woven furniture inspired by the 1925 catalog. Collaborations with avant-garde architects and designers also challenged him to introduce new materials. Metal, a favorite during 1990s minimalism—as testified by the designs of Francesco Bettoni, Mario Cananzi, Carlo Colombo, and Giorgio Ragazzini—blended with rattan core under Mario's art direction, resulting in a powerful design collection.

Mario's ability to look to the future by reexamining the past is highlighted by his longstanding collaboration with Federico Forquet. Born in 1931, this Neapolitan designer worked briefly for Cristóbal Balenciaga in Paris before taking the haute couture world by storm in the 1960s with his toga dresses and nude look. In 1972 (the same year Mario made his debut in the family company), Forquet abandoned the fashion world and turned his passions to interior decoration. A true connoisseur of the classical world and of the arts and crafts it inspired, the decorator has left his mark in palatial interiors and royal abodes alike.

Forquet's collaborations with Bonacina include the furnishings for the rooftop bar Terrazza Martini in Milan and the Caruso hotel in Ravello as well as dozens of private homes, including several belonging to Gianni and Marella Agnelli. Most of the woven pieces he commissioned for these projects were customized. The designers work together instinctively—when Forquet is inspired to create a new piece, he describes his idea to Mario, who brings Forquet's vision to life. "Mario has the extraordinary ability to transform my requests into beautiful objects," Forquet says in an interview for this book. Their collaboration, which has lasted for more than fifty years, also includes textiles, ever since the company acquired the exclusive use of three archival textiles that Forquet designed in the 1970s for Ratti, in Como. Bonacina and Forquet also collaborated on the Futurliberty project, a line of textiles inspired by the early twentieth-century Italian Futurist movement and produced by Liberty London. Launched during the 2023 Design Week in Milan, these new textiles have been used to upholster several Bonacina pieces, including the *Oscar* armchair, a design that was adapted by Margherita Bonacina with Federico Forquet from a model in Giovanni's 1920s catalog.

MATTIA BONETTI

Bonacina's recent history has been defined by an extraordinary collaboration with Paris-based artist and designer Mattia Bonetti. Born in Lugano, Switzerland, in 1952, Bonetti began his career as a textile designer, then expanded into interior and furniture design after he met French designer Elizabeth Garouste in the late 1970s. The pair's unique imaginative design language, infused with primitive elements, set the pace for cutting-edge Parisian design and became synonymous with the most sophisticated contemporary interiors and furniture.

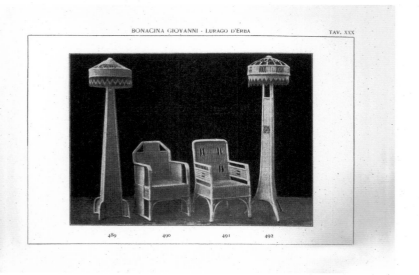

BONACINA GIOVANNI · LURAGO D'ERBA   TAV. XXX

489   490   491   492

Bonetti, whose pieces blur the boundaries between art, craft, and design,
first came to Mario in the early twenty-first century with a monumental
proposal: to create made-to-measure furnishings for the home of an
important client whose name had to remain a secret. "Custom projects
are not new to us," says Antonia. "Despite having nearly 200 models in our
collection, we are often asked to create bespoke products or customize
existing ones." The particularity that emerges from collaborating with Mattia
Bonetti, as Mario describes, is encountering a designer with an uncompromising
vision and great humility in the field—"Mattia works side by side with our
artisans and he is interested in learning every aspect of the material."

From a technical point of view, manufacturing Bonetti's furniture line
Senzafine (which translates as *never-ending*) was one of the greatest
challenges of Mario's career. This series—of round and oval tables, and
sofas of various sizes—is defined by the complexity of its structure: single
rattan canes are shaped by hand to form an intricate pattern of tight curves.
Once the structure is completed, every cane had to be wound with tiny
threads of flat rattan core. "As prototypes were being manufactured in
our workshop, the enthusiasm was evident," says Antonia. "Could such a
complex structure be handcrafted using only natural materials?" Antonia
still recalls the relief she felt when she finally saw a big smile appear on
Mario's face. "That smile conveyed to me that he had succeeded. From then
on, everything went smoothly."

PIERANTONIO BONACINA

The acquisition of the brand Pierantonio Bonacina was significant for several reasons. It ensured that the family name would be preserved while bringing with it a rich archive of works by designers who had collaborated with the company: Tito Agnoli, Joe Colombo, Ico Parisi, Gio Ponti, and Marco Zanuso. Pierantonio had already experimented for many years with a synthetic material that perfectly re-created the feeling of a natural material, and the merger allowed that outdoor expertise to be shared.

Gianfranco and Isabella Bonacina were proud to witness the fruit of their labor continuing in the entrepreneurial drive of the fourth Bonacina generation. Elia and Margherita Bonacina took great pride in unifying under the same name, further solidifying the family legacy. The seamless integration of the Pierantonio Bonacina brand into the fold not only added a brand with a rich history in design experimentation and collaboration with renowned designers but also elevated the collective design heritage. This integration fostered a profound sense of unity and continuity in the company's journey, celebrating the past while embracing the future of Bonacina.

GIO PONTI

Born in 1891, Gio Ponti belonged to an older time, yet the multitalented architect; furniture, costume, and set designer; author; and academician participated in the new aesthetic movement propelled by Milan's postwar resurgence. A firm believer in the value of the applied arts and decoration, Ponti supported the work of younger Italian designers. In 1954, he founded the Compasso d'Oro, a prestigious prize, initially sponsored by La Rinascente, that continues to single out and promote the best examples of Italian design. (It is today organized by ADI, the Association for Industrial Design.) Bonacina's products have received many of these prizes.

Ponti appreciated the versatility of Bonacina's woven rattan and asked the company to produce several of his designs, including a minimalist holder for architectural drawings and a multifunctional children's footstool. For his home, Ponti conceived of an elegantly curvaceous rattan armchair with an exquisite silhouette, called *Continuum*. Ponti, an internationalist, may have been inspired for this chair by the 1961 *Life* magazine report about the "Return of Curly, Curvy Wickerwork." But while rattan furniture produced in the United States was imbued with an aura of Victorian nostalgia, Ponti's designs for Bonacina were firmly rooted in a Rationalist aesthetic.

JOE COLOMBO

Bonacina's talent for identifying and attracting avant-garde designers has always been its strength. This is evidenced by the encounter with Joe Colombo, one of the most visionary Italian designers of the 1960s. Before taking the design world by storm with his futuristic approach, Colombo had been a

painter affiliated with the 1950s avant-garde *Movimento Nucleare* (Nuclear Art Movement). As a designer, a career he pursued for nine years until his sudden death in 1971 at the age of forty-one, he is remembered for his modular pieces and his ability to strike a balance between artistic creativity and pure industrial design. He was prophetic. "Designers will no longer just draw with a pencil," Joe Colombo once stated, "but they will create in partnership with technicians, scientists, professors, doctors, and, in the fairly near future, even electronic brains."

In 1964, Bonacina produced the *Nastro* armchair, a streamlined design made of rattan. For Joe Colombo, who was used to working with the most technological of materials available, producing this futuristic piece using natural rattan, which at that time still bore nostalgic connotations, was a challenge he gladly accepted.

The result is an experimental piece that marks Colombo's longing to distance himself from the modernist form-follows-function principle. With *Nastro*, he embraced a freer and far more dynamic approach to lifestyle and interior design, one he hoped would ultimately "allow us to live in tune with the present and create a viable future."

PIERO LISSONI AND CONTEMPORARY PROJECTS

Other flowerings sprouted from the collaboration with Piero Lissoni, one of the masters of contemporary design and the founder of Lissoni Associati, a multidisciplinary company with studios in Milan and New York. The collaboration with Piero Lissoni led to the creation of noteworthy pieces. Although Lissoni has created some of Bonacina's most classic twenty-first-century rattan pieces, characterized by refined simplicity in the architect's signature style, he has also paved the way for other materials. One of them is the resilient Iroko wood from the west coast of Africa. The result of this collaboration is three lines of streamlined furniture—all made for indoor and outdoor use.

Other contemporary designers that posed some challenges were Marco Zanuso Jr. and Giuseppe Raboni, with the *Super Elastica* armchair. Making an elastic woven cane structure that could adapt to any body shape or weight required the intrinsic characteristics of rattan, such as elasticity and flexibility. The result, a monolithic shape counterbalanced by an open weave, was so successful when it appeared in 2005 that it was included in the Triennale Design Museum Milan's permanent collection, becoming one of the most iconic pieces of the twenty-first century—and chosen for this book's cover.

Clémentine Chambon's exoskeletal structures, as seen in her 2014 *Elliptic* chair, are similarly defined by the complexity of their weaves. *Elliptic* won the French Design Award in January 2024. "As long as we like a project," says Antonia Bonacina, "we are open to collaborating with everyone, whether it's a well-known name or an emerging designer."

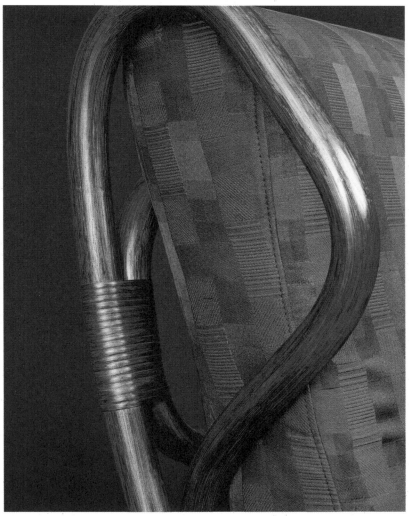

OPPOSITE AND RIGHT
Continuum armchair, 1963,
design by Gio Ponti. In 2023,
on the sixtieth anniversary of its
creation, the design was released
as a special edition by Bonacina,
with textiles from the Rubelli x
Ginori collection.

ABOVE Fiat 500 Spiaggina, Bonacina x Garage Italia custom collaboration. Photographed at Villa Sola Cabiati on Lake Como.

LEFT For this collaboration, Bonacina contributed the hand-woven rattan core seats. Bonacina creates woven seats harmonizing with the bodywork color, which is the true point of innovation compared to the early models made by Vittorio in the 1950s.

BONACINA MUSEUM

The Bonacina Museum was inaugurated in February 2023. Center stage is the craftsmanship that lies behind every design. All the star pieces are there: Franco Albini's *Margherita* and *Gala* armchairs, from 1951; Franca Helg's 1967 *Primavera* armchair; Joe Colombo's 1964 *Nastro* armchair and sofa; Giovanni Travasa's organic shapes from the 1960s, such as the *Palla*, *Eva*, *Eureka*, and *Foglia* armchairs. These icons, alongside never-before-seen works by Raffaella Crespi, Gianfranco Frattini, Ico Parisi, and Gio Ponti, bear witness to Bonacina's enterprising courage. As does the museum itself, a 1960s building commissioned by Vittorio and Carla Bonacina and designed by architect Lorenzo Forges Davanzati, a longtime Bonacina collaborator and an architect of great human and cultural depth. The asymmetric glass-and-concrete structure is a tribute to brutalist architecture and offers a total immersion in the history and legacy of this company. "Our archive collection," says Antonia Bonacina, "reminds us of our enduring passion for innovation." Now that the fourth Bonacina generation has made its grand entrance, with Elia at the helm of the company and Margherita flanking her father in design, the spirit of innovation is experiencing a rebirth. "We are a historic company with the energy of a start-up," says Elia.

RECENT PROJECTS

After acquiring Pierantonio Bonacina, the company expanded its outdoor collection with a line of woven furniture made with state-of-the-art materials created specifically for their resilience. The outdoor line helped propel the company into new scenarios. The 2023 Spiaggina project, in collaboration with Garage Italia, has roots that go back to the 1960s, when Vittorio Bonacina was commissioned by the Agnelli family to furnish the interiors of some Fiat 500 and 600 cars using woven rattan. Garage Italia has expanded on that theme by taking original Fiat 500s, removing the tops, and replacing the combustion engines with electric ones. Once the shells were completed, they commissioned Bonacina to redesign the cars' interiors, with Elia's brilliant intuition of using pastel-colored woven rattan to complement the exteriors.

Recently Bonacina unveiled an innovative and ambitious project that brings weaving to a new frontier in design. The new kitchen, created in collaboration with designer Ronen Joseph, is inspired by the sinuous lines of naval designs and reveals the versatility and technical resistance of the material it is made of.

"Our main inspiration came from the nautical world. In order to obtain its organic shapes, we spent a long time creating the molds that would allow the dense pith fabric to adhere perfectly to the irregular surface. Our work and experimentation was very similar to that of tailored projects," says Ronen Joseph. "We have been experimenting together for several years, investigating how far Bonacina could go. In particular,

we have been thinking together about ideas for products that have not yet been explored."

Compared to its traditional production, Bonacina's main innovation in this new project was to create an extremely complex system of components, topped with a material that is not usually seen in the kitchen world.

"This particular kitchen concept almost started for fun as we were going through the Bonacina archives, searching for products that had been tailor-made for large hotels or special projects that had never seen the light of day. With the restyling of our showroom and the inauguration of the Museo Galleria Giardino—which houses the museum and spaces for the display of indoor and outdoor furniture—we wanted to add this new element to our collections: a kitchen made by Bonacina that would demonstrate our ability to create very distinctive products within the world of furniture while still maintaining our unequivocal style," says Elia Bonacina.

CONCLUSION

If Giovanni Bonacina, the man who founded this company in 1889 at the age of twenty, could see what it has become, what would his reaction be? Elia pondered just a few seconds before replying with a bright smile. "He would approve! After all, we have remained true to his core ethos, which was to honor the past by remaining curious, inventive, and fearless in embracing the future. No matter how much the world continues to change, the hope of each and every one of us is that future generations of our family will continue to weave new and beautiful Bonacina stories."

PRECEDING PAGES On the patio of the Museo Galleria Giardino are *Palla* armchairs, 1966, design by Giovanni Travasa, now modified for outdoor use.

OPPOSITE Bas-relief by d'Amico, dated 1963, is located in the entryway of the Bonacina Museum at the Museo Galleria Giardino, Lurago d'Erba. For the opening, Vittorio Bonacina commissioned the work of art, which was originally on the facade of the building.

267

OPPOSITE A glimpse of interacting spaces at the Museo Galleria Giardino. The 1960s architecture of Lorenzo Forges Davanzati has been carefully preserved.

BELOW Overscale weavings at the windows of the Bonacina Museum represent some of the most iconic Bonacina patterns. The works were realized by Studio unPIZZO in collaboration with Margherita Bonacina.

FOLLOWING PAGES One of Bonacina's recent, and most ambitious, projects is a kitchen designed in collaboration with Ronen Joseph.

ACKNOWLEDGMENTS

We extend our heartfelt gratitude to all the individuals and organizations whose contributions brought this book to life.

First and foremost, immense appreciation goes to the gracious owners of the breathtaking locations showcased within these pages. Your generosity in opening your spaces allowed us to capture the essence of beauty and sophistication that defines our brand. Without your magical spaces, our products would not shine as brightly.

A heartfelt shout-out goes also to the hotels that opened up their doors, allowing us to photograph their halls, patios, and communal areas. Your warm hospitality played a vital role in creating the ambiance we sought to convey.

To the brilliant architects and talented interior designers who continually choose our brand, we extend our sincerest thanks. And to our clients, whose unwavering trust has been the cornerstone of our success: we extend our heartfelt gratitude for continuing to believe in the vision initiated by Giovanni Bonacina in 1889, then guided by the dynamic spirit of Vittorio and later by his son Mario with a blend of rationalism and decorative finesse, now evolves under the youthful innovation of Elia, steering the firm toward new horizons and challenges.

Our gratitude extends to Rizzoli and Studio NR2154, for their unwavering support and professionalism throughout this journey.

A special mention to Marella Caracciolo Chia for her invaluable insights into our brand and its unique way of telling stories.

We extend our thanks to Guido Taroni for his innovative way of being a photographer, always adding a playful perspective and personal touch, which breathed new life into our book. Working together is a true privilege.

We owe a debt of gratitude to Martin Westlake for his daring photography, capturing the essence of our sourcing locations. Your brave dedication—even in the face of a tropical hurricane—has immortalized the special allure that inspires our work.

To Filippo Ferrarese, a talented architect and photographer, thank you for your keen eye and meticulous attention to detail. Your contributions bring our vision to life with stunning beauty.

Lastly, to all the individuals at Bonacina who meticulously reviewed this book, investing so much time to achieve this outstanding result, we extend our sincerest thanks.

To everyone who played a part, no matter how big or small, in the creation of this book, we offer our deepest gratitude. Your support and dedication have truly made a difference.

THE BONACINA FAMILY AND COMPANY

First published in the United States of America in 2024 by
Rizzoli International Publications, Inc.
300 Park Avenue South
New York, New York 10010
rizzoliusa.com

Publisher: Charles Miers
Senior Editor: Philip Reeser
Production Manager: Alyn Evans
Copy Editor: Claudia Bauer
Managing Editor: Lynn Scrabis

Design by NR2154

Text by Marella Caracciolo Chia
Foreword by Madison Cox
Introduction by Elia Bonacina

ISBN: 978-0-8478-3610-9
Library of Congress Control Number: 2024936364

2024 2025 2026 2027 / 10 9 8 7 6 5 4 3 2 1

Printed in Italy

All images copyright © by Guido Taroni except for those on the following pages:
167–69: Ngoc Minh Ngo
171–75: Nicolas Mathéus
196–205: Martin Westlake
208–9, 234, 253, 257, 260, 268–69: Filippo Ferrarese
220: Roberta Bruno for *Forbes*
226–29, 235, 237–38, 240, 242, 244–49, 252, 255: Bonacina Historical Archive
250: LaPresse / Alamy Stock Photo

FSC
www.fsc.org
MIX
Paper | Supporting
responsible forestry
FSC® C084761